the future of literacy

THE HUMAN FUTURES SERIES

Barry N. Schwartz and Robert Disch,
General Editors

ROBERT DISCH, a general editor of the Human Futures series, currently teaches in the Institute for Older Adults at New York City Community College. He has written, edited, and co-edited a number of volumes, including *White Racism, Hard Rains,* and *The Ecological Conscience.*

When a disciple asked what he would do first to reform the State, Confucius replied:

. . . correct language. . . . If language is not correct, then what is said is not what is meant; if what is said is not what is meant, then what ought to be done remains undone; if this remains undone, morals and art will deteriorate; if morals and art deteriorate, justice will go astray; if justice goes astray, the people will stand about in helpless confusion. Hence there must be no arbitrariness in what is said. This matters above everything.

—*Analects* 13:3

1. *Take any scrap of writing. Whichever one comes to hand. A page from a dictionary or a telephone book; a press clipping; an ad; one of Shakespeare's sonnets; a list of books; street names; a Latin sentence.*
2. *Take another scrap.*
3. *Etc.*
4. *Cut up each scrap or recopy it.*
5. *Choose a title (optional).*
6. *Arrange each scrap on a clean page.*
7. *Stop when you've had enough.*
8. *The result will be "texts."*
   (In this manner you will have made "texts.")

—Jacques Ehrmann

the future
of literacy

EDITED BY *Robert Disch*

PRENTICE-HALL, INC. *Englewood Cliffs, N.J.*
A SPECTRUM BOOK

Library of Congress Cataloging in Publication Data

DISCH, ROBERT, comp.
The future of literacy.

(A Spectrum Book. The Human futures series)
Bibliography: p.
CONTENTS: Charbonnier, G. "Primitive" and
"civilized" peoples: a conversation with Claude
Lévi-Strauss.—Havelock, E. Poetry as preserved
communication.—McLuhan, M. The printed word:
architect of nationalism. [etc.]
1. Communication—Addresses, essays, lectures.
2. Books and reading—Addresses, essays, lectures.
I. Title.
P91.D5   301.2   73–12224
ISBN 0–13–346023–1
ISBN 0–13–346015–0 (pbk.)

10 9 8 7 6 5 4 3 2 1

PRENTICE-HALL INTERNATIONAL, INC. (*London*)
PRENTICE-HALL OF AUSTRALIA PTY. LTD. (*Sydney*)
PRENTICE-HALL OF CANADA LTD. (*Toronto*)
PRENTICE-HALL OF INDIA PRIVATE LIMITED (*New Delhi*)
PRENTICE-HALL OF JAPAN, INC. (*Tokyo*)

For Anna and Ellawyn

contents

the future of literacy

introduction

Twenty-four centuries before Marshall McLuhan announced the terminal phase of print culture in *The Gutenberg Galaxy* and *Understanding Media,* Plato had made strikingly prophetic observations regarding some of the drawbacks of alphabetic literacy: A book, Socrates argued in the *Phaedrus,* is always vulnerable to misunderstandings, especially when read by someone who is unprepared for its complexities. Unlike spoken dialogue, which is subject to constant correction, a book is mute; it cannot defend itself against misinterpretation, clarify terminology, or repair deficiencies in logic. Words, like the figures in realistic paintings, "stand before us as though they were alive." But if we attempt to question a book about its meaning, the "words go on telling [us] the same things forever." Because of these limitations, he warned, teachers who rely on writing will breed pedantic students who appear wise because they know many facts, but who "for the most part know nothing" of true wisdom.

Anticipating the concerns of Harold Adams Innis, McLuhan, and other communications specialists, Socrates realized that new techniques and inventions have unpredictable and often undesirable side effects. "To one it is given to create the things of art," he said, "and to another to judge what measure of harm or profit they have for those that shall employ them." [1] Such, he claimed, was the case with writing —still a relatively new technique in fourth-century Athens.

In this brief reference to writing Socrates was apparently concerned more with the effects of the *abuse* of literacy than with specific drawbacks *inherent* in the processes of reading and writing. As the

[1] R. Hackforth, trans. *Plato's Phaedrus* (Cambridge, England: Cambridge University Press, 1952), pp. 156–62.

contents of this book reveal, after post-Gutenberg technologies and other developments made possible the rise of mass literacy, modern critics would discover dangers in literacy and literary culture far more radical than those suggested by Socrates.

It is easy to forget that mass literacy as we know it today is an extremely recent event in history. For 500,000 years human life went on without any known form of ideographic or phonetic literacy. In the time of ancient Greece and Rome, books were limited in number and often read aloud by slaves or servants; the silent, solitary reading habits characteristic of modern literacy were not widely practiced until after the advent of the printing press.[2] Carlo Cipolla reminds us, in *Literacy and Development in the West,* that even as late as 1750 "more than 90 percent of the world's population had no access to the art."

During the eighteenth century, however, a number of factors converged to give birth to the movement toward universal literacy. One was the growth of the bourgeoisie, which since the previous century in England had been pressing hard on the heels of the aristocracy for political, economic, and cultural power. Literacy became a distinguishing characteristic of the aspiring middle classes; it not only separated the middle-class individual from his lower-class origins, but also provided a convenient tool with which to conduct commerce, amass capital, and exercise power. It is not surprising that the great middle-class novels of Defoe and Richardson—as well as the formal grammar book—appeared while this class was searching for ways to establish its values, confirm its identity, and define its role in the world. Furthermore by the end of the eighteenth century, England required a large, literate bureaucracy to administer its growing empire. The raw materials obtained from the colonies, in turn, helped fuel the industrial revolution. "As technology progressed," writes Carlo Cipolla, "the demand for literate, well-trained labor increased." Another factor was the crucial function the Reformation had earlier assigned to literacy in the drama of salvation. Protestant schools emphasized reading so that students could discover for themselves the moral and ethical teachings of the Bible.

As these parallel and interdependent tendencies developed throughout the eighteenth and nineteenth centuries, the lingering class and religious biases against the spread of literacy were largely overcome, as were the fears of some that reading "fictions" would lead to moral corruption.

By the middle of the nineteenth century, when literacy rates in

---

[2] Jack Goody, ed., *Literacy in Traditional Societies* (Cambridge, England: Cambridge University Press, 1968), p. 42.

England were approaching 70 percent, the assumption that literacy and progress were identical had become a dogma of progressive thought. Many thinkers believed that universal literacy was no less than the final milestone on the road to Utopia. They argued that by attaining access to competing ideas and proposals, mankind would benefit from the best of possible choices.

If literacy had great functional value in the minds of some nineteenth-century thinkers, for others it was useful as an antidote to the poisonous spiritual climate that seemed to accompany progress. For Matthew Arnold literature was a vessel that could contain and preserve the "best that had been thought and written" in a world where human values were disintegrating under the onslaught of rapid change. Sensitive to the ugliness of industrialization, repelled by claims that human and material progress were the same, and depressed by cultural fragmentation and deadening "scientific" views of the universe, Arnold believed that literature had the power to "bind life afresh into a whole."

Along with many other writers and critics, Arnold endowed literature with a quasi-religious function at a time when the religious basis of Western culture was suffering irreparable damage. These authors saw in literature and literary culture a spiritual anchor for a world adrift in a sea of change.

Subsequently the twentieth century inherited a mystique of literacy born out of the two tendencies. One, essentially utilitarian, was committed to the functional uses of literacy as a medium for the spread of practical information that could lead to individual and social progress; the other, essentially aesthetic and spiritual, was committed to the uses of literacy for salvaging the drooping spirit of Western man from the death of religion and the ravages of progress. While these tendencies were easily distinguished at their extremes (e.g., a cookbook and a poem by Hopkins), they were not so easily divided at the point of popular novels, journalism, and nonfiction writings. At the present time, when the distinctions are even more difficult—if not impossible—to make, both the "utilitarian" and "spiritual-aesthetic" uses of literacy are attacked as insufficient—if not hostile—to the requirements of either purpose.

THE CASE AGAINST PHONETIC LITERACY

While most nineteenth-century intellectuals and social prophets believed that literacy—in both its utilitarian and its spiritual domains —was an unmitigated good, a few more skeptical critics followed Socrates and suggested that literacy might have undesirable effects. In the early seventeenth century, Francis Bacon thought that the spread of modern languages would "at one time or another play the bankrupt with books." For Alexander Pope, who wrote in the eighteenth century when literacy rates in England were below 20 percent, the proliferation of printed matter already threatened to destroy the Christian-humanist literary tradition that he and his friend Swift equated with civilization and culture. According to McLuhan, "Pope's *Dunciad* proclaims the effects of Gutenberg technology first as a retriever of ancient learning and then as the agent of distraction of all learning. Saturation by ink blacked out the minds that had at first found in the printed page the 'inner light'."

The inky smog that Pope found settling over the modern psyche and driving out the best writers from the cultural heritage was thought by Nietzsche, in the nineteenth century, to have turned modern man into "a walking encyclopedia" who "carries inside an enormous heap of indigestible knowledge—stones that occasionally rattle together in his body."

The prophetic imagination of these writers is confirmed by the glut of print which today demeans literacy and threatens its future. Ironically, print's greatest virtue—its capacity to preserve information through space and time—has become one of its deadly vices. In non-literate societies, where much information had to be transmitted by word of mouth, a "structural amnesia" concerning the past was unavoidable since only so much material could be physically remembered or was considered worth remembering.

In literate societies, trillions of words are preserved regardless of value, and billions are added to the heap each year. It is estimated that more books will be produced between 1973 and 1990 than have previously been written so far in history.

Arnold's dream of a literary tradition that could supplement or replace religion depended upon the existence of "great men of culture," those who labor to "divest knowledge of all that [is] harsh, uncouth, difficult, abstract, professional, exclusive; to humanize it, to make it efficient outside the clique of the cultivated and learned, yet still remaining the best knowledge and thought of the time. . . ." However, the necessity for today's scholars and men of letters to digest millions of written words in order to claim mere competency in their fields undoubtedly suffocates creative scholarship, forces specialization, and renders absurd Arnold's conception of the ideal man of culture.

Some imaginative scholars have, in fact, actually welcomed the opportunity to work without the inhibiting presence of previous scholarship. Eric Auerbach, one of the great literary scholars of the twentieth century, wrote his finest book, *Mimesis,* during World War II in Istanbul where scholarly references were almost nonexistent. "If it had been possible," he observed at the conclusion of *Mimesis,* "for me to [have acquainted] myself with all the work that [had] been done . . . I might never have reached the point of writing."

Shortly before he died, while teaching at Yale, Auerbach found that he could not read the annual scholarly output on even Dante, let alone that on the other writers from Homer to Woolf he had discussed in *Mimesis.*

Printed glut also makes it extremely difficult for many talented authors to receive the critical attention that helps build a sympathetic following. Although writers have always complained about limited audiences, poor publicity, and exploitation by publishers and agents, in the past they could at least dream that recognition would someday arrive, even if posthumously. Such thoughts motivated Stendahl and Henry James, among others. Today, when each week brings a barrage of new titles and announcements of "significant new voices," it is more difficult than at any time in post-Gutenberg history to believe that one's genius will somehow be spared from oblivion.

Who, in fact, will ever know what insights and subtle realizations are buried in the "briefly noted" and "books received" departments of newspapers and periodicals? Some books will not even be bought by libraries; others will vanish into the dusty stacks never to be heard of again. Even in the universities, where the discovery and development of new talent should be a primary concern, the standard offerings in literature continue to labor the "great books." In contemporary literature courses, well-established writers such as Yeats, Pound, James, Eliot, Joyce, Lawrence, Kafka, Faulkner, and Hemingway, are granted domination over current writers.

The existence of verbal glut and clutter obviously demoralizes writers. In one of his last interviews Blaise Cendrars complained that "You all want us to write books without ever stopping. Where does that lead? Tell me . . . go take a walk through the Bibliothèque Nationale and you will see where that leads, that route. A cemetery. A submerged continent. Millions of volumes given over to the worms. No one knows any longer whose they are. No one ever asks. Terra incognita. It's rather discouraging."

Presented with these obstacles, it is hardly surprising that published and potential authors turn to film and television in the hope of finding a medium more in tune with the times than the sluggish, time-consuming novel.

The accumulation of printed glut is an ineradicable disease of literate culture. And, as with any illness, an unhealthy environment will indicate a less hopeful prognosis. In the United States at the present time, there are a number of built-in factors that are exacerbating the pathology of verbal arteriosclerosis. One is the economics of commercial publishing which requires publishers to present a semi-annual list of books, even if many of the books are of little value. The existence of libraries, in turn, helps make it profitable to publish because libraries have annual budgets to purchase books that are often aimed directly at the library market.

The glut syndrome is also fed by the universities and the university presses. Each year the politics of academe force into publication thousands of "scholarly" books and articles that often have little value beyond enhancing the author's career. Despite the fact that most students, professors, and administrators openly deplore the "publish or perish" mania, there is little evidence that hiring, promotion, and tenure decisions are being made on the more reasonable basis of teaching ability.

THE CRISIS OF HUMANISM

Of greater importance for the future of literacy than the problem of glut are charges made by scores of critics and writers that Western culture—of which literacy and literary traditions are a crucial part—has come to the end of its development and that only through a revolutionary transformation will it be revitalized. The humanistic tradition, it is argued, has failed to provide a bulwark against the political obscenities of the twentieth century. In short, Arnold's dream that a vital tradition of literature and letters could prevent the disintegration of humane values has failed to materialize.

Prior to World War II, it was generally assumed by most educated people that exposure to the humanities in fact "humanized" people. The study of the great books, it was thought, helped develop critical thinking, an awareness of humane values, and a knowledge of the essential brotherhood of mankind.

After World War II, when it became known that many of those involved at all levels of the Nazi movement were as likely as not to be devotees of Goethe, Mozart, Shakespeare, and Nietzsche, and that most German professors of literature had supported Hitler (Goebbels himself had a Ph.D. in literature), the commonplace assumptions about the civilizing influences of the humanities had to be carefully reexamined. "Why," asks literary scholar George Steiner in reference to Nazi Germany, "did humanistic traditions and models of conduct prove so fragile a barrier against political bestiality? In fact, were they a barrier, or is it more realistic to perceive in humanistic culture express solicitations of authoritarian rule and cruelty?"

When, in the early 1960s, a youthful band of professors, deans, and alumni of the best liberal arts colleges—the "new mandarins" and "the best and the brightest" as they were dubbed—came to Washington, D.C., to participate in an administration which was later charged with the initiation, planning, and execution of a war that many believed approached the worst excesses of Nazism, the humanizing effects of humane learning were further called in question.

Not only did it appear that humanistic traditions were powerless to prevent such disillusioning episodes but moreover, as Steiner wrote, humanistic culture might in fact be a *source* of "authoritarian rule and cruelty," an assertion that found agreement throughout the '60s among blacks, Chicanos, Indians, and other minorities in the U.S. For these groups, the Western literary tradition as taught in the universities exemplified the worst kinds of cultural arrogance, racism, and elitism—all masked under the mystifying clichés of the "open mind" and "objective inquiry."

While much of the most strident criticism of humanistic culture came from people like Steiner, Louis Kampf, Paul Lauter, Bruce Franklin, Frederick Crews, and others whose lives had been devoted to the teaching and criticism of literature, many outstanding writers themselves began to doubt the value of writing and literary activity in general. As Cendrars pointed out, the problem of glut, alone, is a massive discouragement to many writers. Earlier in the century, D. H. Lawrence said that "the great masses of the population should never be taught to read or write. . . ." Eugène Ionesco denounced the capacity of written language to do more than obscure the truth; Antonin Artaud, in a series of pronouncements and manifestoes, charged that the written word was one of the most important causes of the death of the theater. "All writing is rubbish" he announced in *The Theater and Its Double,* "The libraries of Alexandria can be burnt down. There are forces above and beyond papyrus. . . ." The list could easily be extended.

To some extent the attacks on literary culture reflected pervasive doubts about the capacity of language to sustain a humanistic tradition and to provide the raw materials for writers to defend humane values. The cruel and destructive events of twentieth-century history suggested to many that language was inadequate to propose humane solutions to the problems of modern life, and that people who placed their faith in words were either deluded or insensitive. "No poetry after Auschwitz," wrote Theodor Adorno. In his essay, "Silence and the Poet," George Steiner describes Kafka's anguish over the "impossibility of adequate statement . . . the hopelessness of the writer's task which is to find language as yet unsullied, worn to cliché, made empty by unmeditated waste."

In many important writings Steiner has attempted to define the relationship between language and culture, and between the corruption of language and the brutal facts of recent history. Although he is vague about the precise nature of the relationship, he does suggest that the collapse of language, through abuse or exhaustion, can lead to barbaric behavior, and that vitality in language might provide a verbal framework to inhibit cultural collapse. Yet Steiner's own investigations of this elusive topic reveal major confusions and difficulties.

In a review of the *Supplement* to the *Oxford English Dictionary* in *The New York Times Book Review,* Steiner argues that the dynamic center of the English language no longer resides in Britain or in "British English." Two major wars, the loss of political and economic power, and the "weight of 1,000 years of conscious history" have drained England of "linguistic force." While Steiner admits the difficulties involved in making distinctions between British and non-British English, he is convinced that American speech contains "a raw precision of imagery, a musical wealth . . . a palpable directness . . . which recall the explosive enhancement of Tudor and Elizabethan English."

But if the corruption of language helped bring about Buchenwald, as Steiner has frequently argued, what facts of linguistic degradation account for the atrocities committed by the United States in Indochina? His inconsistency on this point poses a fundamental and perhaps unanswerable question about the relationship between language and history. If he is correct regarding the vitality of North American (and Australian) English, what occurred in Indochina should not have happened. And if the glory of "British English" evolved in conjunction with a period of imperialistic expansion, endless wars, and drives toward world domination, then we should invert the argument and hope that linguistic vitality develops only within militarily impotent nations. Such perverse reasoning, of course, does more to reveal the inadequacies of making simplistic correlations between language and politics than it does to enlighten us about the nature of a complicated and little-understood relationship.

SYMPTOMS OF DECLINE

There are other, less obvious symptoms of the decline of literacy than the rash of attacks on humanistic culture and the language that supports it. One of the more important of these indicators is the general indifference on the part of established powers in the industrialized West to the contents of books. Much self-censorship is, of course, imposed by writers themselves, as well as by editors, lawyers, and publishers. There is, nevertheless, a freedom from censorship granted books —at least in the United States—that is not allowed most other media.

Once-staid textbook houses today expand their lists to include books that recommend necrophilia, cannibalism of deceased relations, family orgies, and fornication with children; other books, such as *Steal This Book* and *The Anarchist's Cook Book,* tell how to make bombs, zap cops, steal, forge airline tickets, collapse water mains, blow telephone systems, and use slugs, to name a few topics.

By contrast, television operates under such levels of censorship that, as numerous critics have complained for years, its content is, with few exceptions, a cultural and political wasteland ruled over by Lassie and Walter Cronkite. When television does allow a divergent point of view, the dissenting spokesman is normally placed in such a defensive position by his interlocutor, or by a hostile "panel," that his opinions appear to the viewer as those of an aberrant kook, a temporary interruption before the Susskinds, Brinkleys, Cronkites, and other "men of reason" restore ideological decorum. That books, on the other hand, are seldom honored by political or any other kind of censorship, was proved by the wide distribution of *The Little Red Book* and other revolutionary materials during the recent war.

"New information," writes William Kuhns, "does not necessarily threaten an ensconced power elite. But a new medium does." Books are simply too sluggish, too personal, too unwieldy (even if little and red) to worry the governments and commercial institutions that wield power in the Western democracies. In the United States censorship is most effectively directed at television, and then, in descending order of importance, at radio and newspaper journalism, films, "respectable" periodicals (e.g., *Time, Harper's, The Atlantic*), small circulation magazines (e.g., *The Nation* and *New Republic*), little magazines and underground journals (e.g., *I. F. Stone's Weekly*), and, finally, at books, the least censored because the least feared. (This is not, of course, the case in many developing countries, where governments have confiscated *The Red Badge of Courage* and *The Scarlet Pimpernel* because of the political coloration of their titles. Nor is it the case in the Soviet Union, where the government still fears the cultural and ideological impact of books.)

The indifference of the United States Government to material in books and most periodicals was evident throughout the 1960s, when numerous charges were made that information concerning American involvement in Vietnam had been suppressed by the Johnson Administration. Even one of the presidential aspirants, George Romney, claimed himself a victim of Pentagon brainwashing. The charges were certainly true. And yet, although the government had lied to the people and had suppressed pertinent facts, the most important information about the war was always available in print; it simply was buried in books and in little-read sources like *I. F. Stone's Weekly* and *The Nation*.

Unfortunately for humanity, the influence of the upper echelons of the censorship chain prevented the mass media from making this information available to the public-at-large. Hence "freedom of the press" and mass literacy proved meaningless as checks on the abuse of power.

Beyond the indifference of modern power to print is the growing movement toward touch-feel therapies, body awareness groups, communes, and entire therapeutic communities which use the human dialectic recommended by Socrates in the *Phaedrus* as the ultimate source of human knowledge and wisdom. For 300 years books held sway as the final point of reference in matters of truth and wisdom, but today, written materials are often used only to supplement a search for psychic and emotional wholeness that is carried out primarily through group processes and human interaction.

The book, itself, has become only a temporary guide, a quickly dated compendium of information, insight, and theory that must be constantly revised to reflect the changing conditions that affect human development and individual requirements. The author, likewise, is often considered more a compiler of the group's collective wisdom than an insightful genius whose dogmas must be rigidly adhered to by faithful disciples.

Such shifts in sensibility and valuation do not bode well for the future of literacy as a potent cultural and communicative force. "Who knows," wondered R. P. Blackmur, "it may be the next age will not express itself in words . . . at all, for the next age may not be literate in any sense we understand or the last three thousand years understood." While the contents of this book cannot give easy answers to this question, the contributors do succeed in defining the various contexts, influences, and forces that will shape the future of the written word.

PART ONE

the impact
of
literacy

The difficulties involved in understanding the historical impact of literacy are summed up by Jack Goody in *Literacy in Traditional Societies*.

> Considering the importance of writing over the past 5,000 years, and the profound effects it has on the lives of each and all, surprisingly little attention has been given to the way in which it has influenced the social life of mankind. Studies of writing tend to be histories of the development of scripts, while literary scholars concentrate upon the content rather than the implications of communicative acts. And while postwar interest has directed attention to the influence of changing communications on society, most writers have been concerned with later developments such as printing, radio and television. (p. 1)

Since World War II, though, important studies have been undertaken by Harold Adams Innis, Walter Ong, S.J., Eric Havelock, Marshall McLuhan, and others to assess the complex interactions between literacy, history, and culture. The essays in Part One of this volume indicate some of the approaches that scholars in different fields are taking in their investigations of the consequences of literacy from its beginnings to the present time.

In the opening selection, Claude Lévi-Strauss, drawing on his studies of nonliterate societies, places literacy in relation to other revolutionary events in man's early history. For Lévi-Strauss, who believes that there are no superior societies, the development of writing comes "after humanity had already made its most essential and fundamental discoveries." Though experts disagree about the precise reasons behind the origins of writing, Lévi-Strauss links its appearance in both hemispheres to "the establishment of hierarchical societies." By simplifying the bureaucratic problem of maintaining deeds, inventories, genealogies, and other administrative records, writing facilitated the "exploitation of man by man."

With the spread and sophistication of alphabetic (or phonetic) literacy, the ancient cultures of the Mediterranean were subjected to the radical transformations that always follow the introduction of any revolutionary technology. In "Poetry as Preserved Communication," Eric Havelock shows how Plato, writing in fourth-century Athens, recognized that the "oral" or "poetic" state of mind had to be overthrown if Platonic thought and method were to gain ascendency.

In prose composition, still at that time a relatively new technique, Plato found a weapon to use against the hold of conventional wisdom derived mainly from Homeric mythology, which for centuries had been orally transmitted from generation to generation. At the time he composed the *Republic,* as Havelock explains at the end of *Preface to Plato,* "the stage was set . . . for a genius . . . who as a writer but not as a poet would organize once and for all a prose of ideas; who would expound once and for all in writing what the syntax of this prose must be, and who would explore the rules of logic which should govern it" (p. 305).

The necessary genius was found both in Plato and in Aristotle; in their works the unity of thought and experience that characterized the oral tradition was broken down. Thus Plato's attack on "poetry" is actually an attack on the methods and content of orally transmitted "wisdom"; not, as is commonly thought, on the literary form we understand as poetry today.

According to Havelock, "Man's experience of his society, of himself and of his environment was now given separate organized existence in the abstract word." This event was so significant that Europe still lives in the shadow of Plato and Aristotle, "using their language, accepting their dichotomies, and submitting to their discipline of the abstract as the chief vehicle of higher education, even to this day" (p. 305).

While Havelock's argument is not easy for the nonspecialist to follow, in the opinion of most scholars his is one of the best studies of the historical impact of literacy we have. Hence the whole of *Preface to Plato* is essential reading for any student of the past or future of literacy.

If, as Havelock argues, the techniques of phonetic literacy could serve as a weapon against the traditional orality of older societies, it was not until the printing press and the rise of mass literacy that the explosive potential of writing would be fully realized. In "The Printed Word: Architect of Nationalism," McLuhan claims that "typography ended parochialism and tribalism, psychically and socially, both in space and in time. . . . The typographic extension of man brought in nationalism, industrialization, mass markets, and universal literacy. . . ."

Whether or not such great events can be explained solely in terms of communications technology is a point fiercely debated by communications specialists. Nevertheless, recent studies of the impact of literacy on nonliterate cultures support the argument that the acquisition of literacy will radically alter the political and cultural structures of pre- or quasi-literate societies.

In Brazil, for example, where the illiteracy rate is about 26 percent and has been dropping rapidly, a teacher reported that he helped students to write only their first names because he "was afraid that when they learned to write their full names, they would immediately leave for the city" and join the urban unemployed. While recognizing that literacy without economic opportunity is not enough, another Brazilian teacher pointed out that "something worse than plain literacy is to leave the people illiterate."

Throughout Asia, Africa, and South America, the growth of literacy is unquestionably raising expectations and generating revolutionary awareness. But the transition to full literacy, as anthropologist Jack Goody shows in "Literacy and the Non-literate in Ghana," is a painful process that severely disrupts established custom and creates acute class distinctions.

Ironically while much of the world is presently experiencing the impact of mass literacy, media prophets in the West are announcing the death of print as an effective vehicle for communication in the electronic age—a subject that will occupy the following parts of this book.

Chapter 1

'primitive' and 'civilized' peoples:

a conversation

with Claude Lévi-Strauss

Georges Charbonnier

GEORGES CHARBONNIER. . . . . It is to the anthropologist first and fore-most that we want to put the following question: what are the basic functional and structural differences that you observe between the societies which you study and the society in which we live? . . .

CLAUDE LÉVI-STRAUSS. I am going to put forward an initial hypothesis: in doing so, I confess that I am playing the devil's advocate, since I will not bide by it, but it seems to me that we should begin by considering it as a possibility.

Suppose an inveterate roulette player sets out not only to pick the lucky number, but to work out a very complex combination dependent on, say, ten or a hundred previous spins of the wheel, and determined by certain rules regarding the alternation of red and black, or even and odd numbers. This complex combination might be achieved right away, or at the thousandth or millionth attempt or never at all. Yet it would never occur to us to say that, had he accomplished his combination only at the seven hundred and twenty-fifth attempt, all the previous attempts were indispensable to his success. He was successful at that particular moment, but the moment might well have come later, and that was only how things turned out;

"'Primitive' and 'Civilized' Peoples: A Conversation with Claude Lévi-Strauss" (editor's title). From Georges Charbonnier, *Conversations with Claude Lévi-Strauss*, trans. by John and Doreen Weightman (London: Jonathan Cape Ltd., 1969), excerpted from pp. 24–31. Original title was "'Primitive' Peoples and 'Civilized' Peoples." English translation, copyright © 1969 by Jonathan Cape Ltd. Reprinted by permission of Jonathan Cape Ltd. and Grossman Publishers.

yet during the initial attempts there was no progress which might have been considered as the necessary pre-condition of his success. And I might use the analogy in order to reply to the question you put to me a short while ago. Let us say, then, that it was necessary to wait a few hundred thousand years before that most complex combination —western civilization—came into being. Mankind might have achieved the combination at an early stage, or might have done so very much later, but the fact is that it has achieved it at this particular moment, and there is no reason why this should be so, it just is. However, you may say: "That is not very satisfactory."

G.C. No, it does not strike me as being satisfactory. As a non-specialist, I look upon the time factor as being important.

C.L.-S. I would agree with you, but let us try to define the time factor more closely. What does it consist of? I believe that here we must refer to an essential acquisition of culture, which was the pre-condition of that totalization of knowledge and utilization of past experience that we feel, more or less intuitively, to have been the source of our civilization. The cultural acquisition, the conquest, to which I am referring, is writing.

It is certain that a people can only take advantage of previous acquisitions in so far as these have been made permanent in writing. I know, of course, that the societies we call primitive often have a quite staggering capacity for remembering, and we have been told about Polynesian communities who can recite straight off family trees involving dozens of generations; but that kind of feat obviously has its limits. Writing had to be invented so that the knowledge, the experiments, the happy or unhappy experiences of each generation could accumulate, so that, working on the basis of this capital, succeeding generations would be able not only to repeat the same endeavours, but also turn all previous ones to good account in order to improve techniques and achieve fresh progress. Do you agree on this point?

G.C. I think so. I don't see that it is at all debatable.

C.L.-S. Here, then, we have something we can hold on to, since the invention of writing took place in time and space. We know that it occurred in the Eastern Mediterranean some three or four thousand years before the birth of Christ, and that it was a vital discovery.

G.C. But is there something exceptional about the emergence of a phenomenon such as the invention of writing at one particular time and
in one particular place? As a non-specialist, I ask—why there?

C.L.-S. Why there? I may seem to be contradicting what I was suggesting
a moment ago, but I feel that at this point we should introduce a
new idea. Writing appeared in the history of humanity some three or
four thousand years before the beginning of our era, at a time when
humanity had already made its most essential and fundamental discoveries; it appeared not before, but immediately after, what is called
the "neolithic revolution"—the discovery of those civilized skills which
still form the basis of our lives: agriculture, the domestication of animals, pottery-making, weaving—a whole range of processes which were
to allow human beings to stop living from day to day as they had done
in paleolithic times, when they depended on hunting or on the gathering of fruit, and to accumulate . . .

G.C. . . . to build up a reserve stock.

C.L.-S. Yes, precisely, to have a reserve stock. Now, we should be wrong
to think that discoveries as vital as these materialized all at once, and
purely as the result of chance. Agriculture, to take only one example,
represents a mass of knowledge, the accumulated experience of many
generations which was handed down from one to the other before it
became something which could be turned to effective account. It has
often been pointed out that domestic animals are not just wild species
which have become domesticated; they are wild species which have
been completely transformed by man, and this transformation, which
was the necessary pre-condition of man's ability to use them, must
have occupied long periods of time and called for great persistence and
prolonged and concentrated experimentation. Now all that was possible without the existence of writing.
    Therefore, although writing seemed to us a moment ago to be
a pre-condition of progress, we must never lose sight of the fact that
certain essential forms of progress, perhaps the most essential ever
achieved by humanity, were accomplished without the help of writing.

G.C. But we are inevitably led to ask ourselves the same question with
regard to each of these instances of progress. As non-scientists, we
wonder why a particular kind of progress occurred in a particular
place, and the farther back in time I go, the more frequently the
question arises.

c.l.-s. The problem is not quite the same in connection with the neolithic era.

g.c. But the question still remains: what are the underlying conditions of any instance of progress?

c.l.-s. Yes, but it is by no means certain that the major conquests of the neolithic age occurred in one place and at one moment in time. It is even likely that in certain conditions—and some attempt has been made to define them: the relative isolation of human communities living in narrow mountain valleys with the advantage of natural irrigation, and protected by their isolated situation from invasion by foreign populations—the discoveries of the neolithic age occurred independently in different regions of the world. Whereas, as far as writing is concerned, the situation would appear to be much clearer: the appearance of writing in our civilization is at least quite definitely localized. And so we must ask ourselves with what other phenomena it is linked. What was happening at the same time as the invention of writing? What accompanied it? What may have conditioned it? In this connection, there is one fact which can be established: the only phenomena which, always and in all parts of the world, seems to be linked with the appearance of writing, and not only in the eastern Mediterranean but also in China in the earliest known period, and even in those regions of America where crude attempts at writing had occurred before the conquest, is the establishment of hierarchical societies, consisting of masters and slaves, and where one part of the population is made to work for the other part.

And when we consider the first uses to which writing was put, it would seem quite clear that it was connected first and foremost with power: it was used for inventories, catalogues, censuses, laws and instructions; in all instances, whether the aim was to keep a check on material possessions or on human beings, it is evidence of the power exercised by some men over other men and over worldly possessions.

g.c. Social control of power.

c.l.-s. A check on power and at the same time the means by which power was regulated. We have followed a somewhat tortuous route; starting from the problem of progress, we saw that it was connected with the capitalization or totalization of knowledge. This process itself only appeared possible after the point at which writing came into existence, and writing itself, in the first instance, seemed to be associated in any permanent way only with societies which were based on the exploitation of man by man. Therefore, the problem of progress becomes more complicated and appears two-dimensional, instead of uni-dimensional; for if, in order to establish his ascendancy over nature, man had to subjugate man and treat one section of mankind as an object, we can no longer give a simple and unequivocal answer to the questions raised by the concept of progress.

Chapter 2

poetry as preserved communication

Eric Havelock

If we now look back over what has been said in the two previous chapters [of *Preface to Plato*] it can be seen that in Plato's pages [in *The Republic*] the Greek poets play a series of roles which are hard to explain. Perhaps Plato is trying to tell us something about them which is more important than has been realised, but if so, what is it? Somehow their presence seems to brood over his long argument as though they were a persistent obstacle which might cut him off from contact with his public or pupils, and bar the way to Platonism.

However, our examination of what he says about them has not really revealed the reason for this feeling. The problems it has exposed are as follows:

First, why is it that poetry is treated as though it held a monopoly in the present educational apparatus?

Second, why can the works of Homer and the tragedians be treated not as though they were art but as though they were a vast encyclopedia containing information and guidance for the management of one's civic and personal life?

Third, why is Plato so absolutely determined to exclude poetry altogether from higher education, rather than grant it at least a minor role at this level?

Fourth, why as he applies the term *mimesis* to poetry and examines its implications does he seem to assume that the artist's "act" of creation, the performer's "act" of imitation, the pupil's "act" of

"Poetry as Preserved Communication." From Eric Havelock, *Preface to Plato* (Cambridge: Harvard University Press, 1963), pp. 36–49. (Footnotes have been omitted.) Copyright 1963 by the President and Fellows of Harvard College. Reprinted by permission of Harvard University Press and Basil Blackwell Publisher.

learning, and the adult's "act" of recreation all overlap each other? Why are these situations so confused and jumbled up together?

Fifth, why can he apply the *mimesis* now to drama and now to epic, and think that the genre distinction between them does not matter?

Sixth, why is he so frequently obsessed with the psychology of response as it is experienced by the audience? In his description of the emotional impact of poetry he seems often to be describing an almost pathological situation. At least he is exposing an intensity of response in Greek students and in Greek audiences which to us is unfamiliar.

These questions cannot all be answered at once, but they form a connected pattern and lead to a set of conclusions which as they are taken together illuminate the general character of the Greek cultural condition and begin to unlock some of the secrets of the Greek mind. Let us begin by noticing the rather obvious fact, implicit in problems five and six, that Plato finds it difficult to discuss poetry or make any statements about it without discussing also the conditions under which it is performed. This is strikingly true of the first exposition of *mimesis* in Book Three; it is equally true of the more advanced and drastic critique in Book Ten. The actual performance of poetry, we conclude, was far more central to the Greek cultural pattern than we would normally conceive to be the case. It is not just a matter of selected readings given in public or private nor of annual festivals in the theatre. On the contrary the fact that the situation of the learner on the one hand and of the adult on the other are treated without firm distinction implies that performance of poetry was fundamental in adult recreation: that the two situations in Plato's eyes were somehow serving the same end. The class who sat under the harpist and the audience who attended either an epic recital or a performance in the theatre were partners in a general and common practice.

The plain conclusion of this is that performance means oral performance. These people young and old did not habitually read books either for instruction or for amusement. They did not digest an item of information at a desk nor did they acquire their knowledge of Homer and of drama by buying the *Iliad* or a play and taking it home to read. The testimony of Plato already reviewed allows no other conclusion. And it is supported by that vocabulary in which he casually and repeatedly discusses the situation of the poet in his society. As we have seen, when the mighty argument opens in Book Two, the poets are discovered in the foreground of the discussion. After an interval they return to it and submit to censorship of matter and of style, in Books Two and Three. And then in Book Five their influence appears in the background as the opponent of philosophy, and in Book Ten they are dissected and damned. In all these discussions, over and over again, the relationship of the student or the public to poetry is assumed to be that of listeners, not readers, and the relationship of the poet to his public or his constituency is always that of a reciter and/or an actor, never of a writer. The instances are too numerous to mention. One can be cited which happens to be striking. To open the polemic of Book Ten Plato characterises the offence of poetry as fundamental. Why is this? Because it "cripples the intellect," but he adds "the intellect of the listeners," and the addition, so unnecessary from our standpoint, bespeaks the unconscious assumption that even the intellectual influence of poetry, negative as it is, is mediated only in oral performance.

It is fair to conclude that the cultural situation described by Plato is one in which oral communication still dominates all the important relationships and valid transactions of life. Books of course there were, and the alphabet had been in use for over three centuries, but the question is: used by how many? and used for what purposes? Up to this point its introduction had made little practical difference to the educational system or to the intellectual life of adults. This is a hard conclusion to accept, not least in the eyes of scholars of the written word. For they themselves work with reference books and documents and find it correspondingly difficult to imagine a culture worthy of the name which did not. And in fact when they turn their attention to the problem of written documentation they betray a consistent tendency to press the positive evidence for it as far as they can and as far back as they can. However, allowing for this unconscious prejudice, does it not still remain true that the Greeks had been using the alphabet since the eighth century? Are there not a wealth of inscriptions? What of the public decrees inscribed and put up in Athens in the fifth century? What of the references to the use of documents in Old Comedy? Did not the reform, fairly recent when Plato wrote, which converted the Attic alphabet to the Ionic model presuppose a widespread use of documentation? As to the educational curriculum, does not Plato himself in his *Protagoras,* written presumably earlier than the *Republic,* supply the *locus classicus* which attests the teaching of letters in school? These are a sample of the objections which could be cited against the conclusion that Greek culture at the turn of the century was still essentially oral.

Yet the weight of Plato's testimony is there, impossible to shake off, and once one becomes ready to accept it, one becomes prepared also to notice how complicated may be the problem of the growth of Greek literacy and how slippery the evidence which bears on the subject. It is in the first instance to be realised that the habit of public inscription does not necessarily imply popular literacy: it might imply its opposite; nor do the writing habits of Greek poets—for after Homer undoubtedly their works were composed in writing—prove it either. In each case we may be dealing with a situation best described as craft literacy, in which the public inscription is composed as a source of referral for officials and as a check upon arbitrary interpretations. As for the poet, he can write for his own benefit and thereby can acquire increased compositional skill, but he composes for a public who he knows will not read what he is composing but will listen to it. The clue to the whole problem lies not in the use of written characters and writing materials, on which scholarly attention has been concentrated, but upon the supply of readers, and this depended on a universalisation of letters. The reading trauma, to use a modern term, had to be imposed at the primary level of schooling, and not the secondary. As late as the first half of the fifth century the evidence, we suggest, points to the fact that Athenians learnt to read if at all, in adolescence. The skill was imposed upon a previous oral training, and perhaps one learned to write little more than one's signature—the first thing one would want to write—and at that, spelling and orthography were erratic. There is a passage in the *Clouds,* dating from 423 B.C. or later, in which the boys' school presided over by the harpist is described. This omits any reference to letters and stresses oral recitation. It is written in nostalgic vein and, when compared with the statement of the *Protagoras* that children learned their letters in school, permits the inference that in Attic schools the introduction of letters at the primary level as a standardised practice had begun by the beginning of the last third of the fifth century. Such a conclusion is consistent with the achievement of general literacy toward the end of the war, a condition to which the *Frogs* in 405 called attention. Indeed, this last piece of testimony should remind us that Old Comedy not infrequently, if it introduces the use of written documents into some stage situation, tends to treat them as something novel and either comic or suspicious, and there are passages in tragedy which betray the same overtones.

In short, in considering the growing use of letters in Athenian practice, we presuppose a stage, characteristic of the first two-thirds of the fifth century, which we may call semi-literacy, in which writing skills were gradually but rather painfully being spread through the population without any corresponding increase in fluent reading. And if one stops to think about the situation as it existed till near the end of the Peloponnesian war, this was inevitable, for where was the ready and copious supply of books or journals which alone makes fluent reading possible? One cannot build up a habit of popular literacy on a fund of inscriptions. All this makes the testimony of Plato, so inconvenient and yet so weighty, much easier to tolerate, and it becomes the easier if we add the presumption that up to his day the educational apparatus, as so often since, lagged behind technological advance, and preferred to adhere to traditional methods of oral instruction when other possibilities were becoming available. It is only too likely that Plato is describing a situation which was on the way to being changed as he wrote. The testimony of the orators could probably be used to show that by the middle of the fourth century the silent revolution had been accomplished, and that the cultivated Greek public had become a community of readers.

However, for Plato this is not the assumption, nor is he interested in noticing the possibility of change, and for a very fundamental reason. Once it is accepted that the oral situation had persisted through the fifth century, one faces the conclusion that there would also persist what one may call an oral state of mind as well; a mode of consciousness so to speak, and, as we shall see, a vocabulary and syntax, which were not that of a literate bookish culture. And once one admits this and admits that the oral state of mind would show a time lag so that it persisted into a new epoch when the technology of communication had changed, it becomes understandable that the oral state of mind is still for Plato the main enemy.

But we are anticipating what has not yet been demonstrated. Let us ask first the question: assuming a Hellenic social apparatus and a civilisation in which originally there had been no documentation, and then, for three centuries, a situation where documentation remained minimal, how is the apparatus of this civilisation preserved? We speak here of the public and private law of the group, its proprieties and its traditions, its historical sense and its technical skills.

The answer too often supplied to this question, if the question is ever asked, is that the preservation and transmission of the mores is left to the unconscious mind of the community and to the give and take between the generations without further assistance. This in fact, we suggest, is never the case. The "tradition," to use a convenient term, at least in a culture which deserves the name of civilised, always requires embodiment in some verbal archetype. It requires some kind of linguistic statement, a performative utterance on an ambitious scale which both describes and enforces the overall habit pattern, political and private, of the group. This pattern supplies the nexus of the group. It has to become standardised in order to allow the group to function as a group and to enjoy what we might call a common consciousness and a common set of values. To become and remain standardised it has to achieve preservation outside of the daily whim of men. And the preservation will take linguistic form; it will include repeated examples of correct procedure and also rough definitions of standard technical practices which are followed by the group in question, as for example the method of building a house or sailing a ship or cooking food. Furthermore, we suggest, this linguistic statement or paradigm, telling us what we are and how we should behave, is not developed by happy chance, but as a statement which is formed to be drilled into the successive generations as they grow up within the family or clan system. It provides the content of the educational apparatus of the group. This is as true today of literate societies in which the necessary conditioning is acquired through books or controlled by written documents as it was in preliterate society which lacked documents.

In a preliterate society, how is this statement preserved? The answer inescapably is: in the living memories of successive living people who are young and then old and then die. Somehow, a collective social memory, tenacious and reliable, is an absolute social prerequisite for maintaining the apparatus of any civilisation. But how can the living memory retain such an elaborate linguistic statement without suffering it to change in transmission from man to man and from generation to generation and so to lose all fixity and authority? One need only experiment today with the transmission of a single prosaic directive passed down by word of mouth from person to person in order to conclude that preservation in prose was impossible. The only possible verbal technology available to guarantee the preservation and fixity of transmission was that of the rhythmic word organised cunningly in verbal and metrical patterns which were unique enough to retain their shape. This is the historical genesis, the *fons et origo*, the moving cause of that phenomenon we still call "poetry." But when we consider how utterly the function of poetry has altered, how completely the cultural situation has changed, it becomes possible to understand that when Plato is talking about poetry he is not really talking about our kind of poetry.

The probable answers to two of our problems have now already been revealed. If Plato could deal with poetry as though it were a kind of reference library or as a vast tractate in ethics and politics and warfare and the like, he is reporting its immemorial function in an oral culture and testifying to the fact that this remained its function in Greek society down to his own day. It is first and last a didactic instrument for transmitting the tradition. And if secondly he treats it throughout the *Republic* as though it enjoyed in current practice a complete monopoly over training in citizenship he likewise is describing with faithfulness the educational mechanisms of such a culture. The linguistic content had to be poetic or else it was nothing.

And the answers to several other puzzles become apparent if we consider precisely what in an oral culture the educational mechanisms amount to. They cannot be narrowly identified with schools and schoolmasters or with teachers, as though these represented a unique source of indoctrination, as they do in a literate society. All memorisation of the poetised tradition depends on constant and reiterated recitation. You could not refer to a book or memorise from a book. Hence poetry exists and is effective as an educational instrument only as it is performed. Performance by a harpist for the benefit of a pupil is only part of the story. The pupil will grow up and perhaps forget. His living memory must at every turn be reinforced by social pressure. This is brought to bear in the adult context, when in private performance the poetic tradition is repeated at mess table and banquet and family ritual, and in public performance in the theatre and marketplace. The recital by parents and elders, the repetition by children and adolescents, add themselves to the professional recitations given by poets, rhapsodists and actors. The community has to enter into an unconscious conspiracy with itself to keep the tradition alive, to reinforce it in the collective memory of a society where collective memory is only the sum of individuals' memories, and these have continually to be recharged at all age levels. Hence Plato's *mimesis,* when it confuses the poet's situation with the actor's, and both of these with the situation of the student in class and the adult in recreation, is faithful to the facts.

In short, Plato is describing a total technology of the preserved word which has since his day in Europe ceased to exist. Nor have we yet exhausted all the facets of that technology which were peculiar to an oral culture. There remains to consider the personal situation of an individual boy or man who is urgently required to memorise and to keep green in his memory the verbal tradition on which his culture depends. He originally listens and then repeats and goes on repeating, adding to his repertoire to the limits of his mental capacity which naturally will vary from boy to boy and man to man. How is such a feat of memory to be placed within the reach not only of the gifted but of the average member of the group, for all have to retain a minimal grasp of the tradition? Only, we suggest, by exploiting psychological resources latent and available in the consciousness of every individual, but which today are no longer necessary. The pattern of this psychological mechanism will be examined more closely in a later chapter. But its character can be summed up if we describe it as a state of total personal involvement and therefore of emotional identification with the substance of the poetised statement that you are required to retain. A modern student thinks he does well if he diverts a tiny fraction of his psychic powers to memorise a single sonnet of Shakespeare. He is not more lazy than his Greek counterpart. He simply pours his energy into book reading and book learning through the use of his eyes instead of his ears. His Greek counterpart had to mobilise the psychic resources necessary to memorise Homer and the poets, or enough of them to achieve the necessary educational effect. To identify with the performance as an actor does with his lines was the only way it could be done. You threw yourself into the situation of Achilles, you identified with his grief or his anger. You yourself became Achilles and so did the reciter to whom you listened. Thirty years later you could automatically quote what Achilles had said or what the poet had said about him. Such enormous powers of poetic memorisation could be purchased only at the cost of total loss of objectivity. Plato's target was indeed an educational procedure and a whole way of life.

This then is the master clue to Plato's choice of the word *mimesis* to describe the poetic experience. It focuses initially not on the artist's creative act but on his power to make his audience identify almost pathologically and certainly sympathetically with the content of what he is saying. And hence also when Plato seems to confuse the epic and dramatic genres, what he is saying is that any poetised statement must be designed and recited in such a way as to make it a kind of drama within the soul both of the reciter and hence also of the audience. This kind of drama, this way of reliving experience in memory instead of analysing and understanding it, is for him "the enemy."

In conclusion, if one applies these findings to the history of Greek literature before Plato, one is caught up by the proposition that to call it literature in our sense is a misnomer. Homer roughly represents the terminus of a long period of non-literacy in which Greek oral poetry was nursed to maturity and in which only oral methods were available to educate the young and to transmit the group mores. Alphabetic skill was available to a few not later than 700 B.C. Precisely who these few were is a matter of dispute. The circle of alphabet-users became wider as time passed, but what more natural than that previous habits of instruction and of communication along with the corresponding states of mind should persist long after the alphabet had theoretically made a reading culture possible? This leads to the conclusion that all Greek poetry roughly down to the death of Euripides not only enjoyed an almost unchallenged monopoly of preserved communication but also that it was composed under conditions which have never since been duplicated in Europe and which hold some of the secret of its peculiar power. Homer may, for convenience, be taken as the last representative of the purely oral composition. Even this is dubious; it seems improbable that his poems have not benefited from some reorganisation made possible by alphabetic transcription. But this is a controversial point which does not affect the main perspective. It is certain that all his poet successors were writers. But it is equally certain that they always wrote for recitation and for listeners. They composed it can be said under audience control. The advantages of literacy were private to themselves and their peers. The words and sentences they shaped had to be such as were repeatable. They had to be "musical" in a functional sense to which we will later return. And the content had still to be traditional. Bold invention is the prerogative of writers, in a book culture.

In short, Homer's successors still assumed that their works would be repeated and memorised. On this depended their fame and their hope of immortality. And so they also assumed, though in the main unconsciously, that what they should say would be appropriate for preservation in the living memory of audiences. This both restricted their range to the main stream of the Greek tradition and immensely strengthened what might be called the high seriousness of their compositions.

Our business here is not with literary criticism but with the origins of that abstract intellectualism styled by the Greeks "philosophy." We must realise that works of genius, composed within the semi-oral tradition, though a source of magnificent pleasure to the modern reader of ancient Greek, constituted or represented a total state of mind which is not our mind and which was not Plato's mind; and that just as poetry itself, as long as it reigned supreme, constituted the chief obstacle to the achievement of effective prose, so there was a state of mind which we shall conveniently label the "poetic" or "Homeric" or "oral" state of mind, which constituted the chief obstacle to scientific rationalism, to the use of analysis, to the classification of experience, to its rearrangement in sequence of cause and effect. That is why the poetic state of mind is for Plato the arch-enemy and it is easy to see why he considered this enemy so formidable. He is entering the lists against centuries of habituation in rhythmic memorised experience. He asks of men that instead they should examine this experience and rearrange it, that they should think about what they say, instead of just saying it. And they should separate themselves from it instead of identifying with it; they themselves should become the "subject" who stands apart from the "object" and reconsiders it and analyses it and evaluates it, instead of just "imitating" it.

It follows that the history of Greek poetry is also the history of early Greek *paideia*. The poets supply successive supplements to the curriculum. Leadership in education is by Plato accorded successively to Homer, Hesiod, to the tragedians, to the Sophists, and to himself. In the light of the hypothesis that Greece was passing from non-literacy through craft literacy towards semiliteracy and then full literacy, this order makes sense. Epic had been *par excellence* the vehicle of the preserved word throughout the Dark Age. At that time it must also have been the main vehicle of instruction. Even in purely oral form the epic, assisted by the formulaic technique, assumed in part the guise of an authorised version. Once rendered into the alphabet, more rigidly standardised versions became possible for teaching purposes. Tradition associated some school reforms with the age of Solon and some recension of the Homeric text with Pisistratus. It is plausible to connect the two and conclude that what happened, perhaps over an extended period, was an accommodation of written versions to each other for school use. The rhapsodist was also the teacher. He, like the poet—and the two professions overlapped as the career of Tyrtaeus shows—responded to the traditions of craft literacy. He himself used his Homeric text as a reference to correct his memory, but taught it orally to the population at large who memorised but never read it. Like the poet, he also remained under audience control.

But at Athens, under Pisistratus, a second mode of oral composition was given formal status and state support. The Athenian stage plays, composed closer to the native vernacular, became the Attic supplement to Homer as a vehicle of preserved experience, of moral teaching and of historical memory. They were memorised, taught, quoted and consulted. You went to see a new play, but it was at the same time an old play full of the familiar clichés rearranged in new settings, with much aphorism and proverb and prescriptive example of how to behave, and warning examples of how not to behave; with continual recapitulation of bits of tribal and civic history, of ancestral memories for which the artist serves as the unconscious vehicle of repetition and record. The situations were always typical, not invented; they repeated endlessly the precedents and judgments, the learning and wisdom, which the Hellenic culture had accumulated and hoarded.

Plato casually identifies Homer as the archetypal figure for the fundamental reason that his epic was not only the prototype of all preserved communication and remained so; its compendious content and widespread performance provided a continuity within which Greek drama can be seen as imitating the content and adapting the method to a performance which, stylistically speaking, differed in degree rather than in kind, as Plato himself perceived. The Homeric background of tragedy is institutional and fundamental. It is a matter of the expanding technology of the shaped and preserved utterance, whether recited and mimed by an epic rhapsodist who himself "does" all the characters, or split up into parts done by different reciters who become actors. One may add that as this took place, the Attic intelligence was able to demonstrate its superiority over that of other Greek states by adding its own characteristic ingredient to the curriculum. Athenian children and adolescents of the fifth century who included the Greek drama or excerpts thereof in their memorised *paideia* could draw on larger resources than was possible in those communities where Homer may have retained a virtual monopoly.

But the main burden of Plato's attack is on Homer. He occupies the forefront of his mind and it is time to turn to test Plato's conception of Homer the encyclopedist; to test, that is, the hypothesis that this epic archetype of the orally preserved word was composed as a compendium of matters to be memorised, of tradition to be maintained, of a *paideia* to be transmitted.

Chapter 3

the printed word:
architect of nationalism

Marshall McLuhan

"You may perceive, Madam," said Dr. Johnson with a pugilistic smile, "that I am well-bred to a degree of needless scrupulosity." Whatever the degree of conformity the Doctor had achieved with the new stress of his time on white-shirted tidiness, he was quite aware of the growing social demand for visual presentability.

Printing from movable types was the first mechanization of a complex handicraft, and became the archetype of all subsequent mechanization. From Rabelais and More to Mill and Morris, the typographic explosion extended the minds and voices of men to reconstitute the human dialogue on a world scale that has bridged the ages. For if seen merely as a store of information, or as a new means of speedy retrieval of knowledge, typography ended parochialism and tribalism, psychically and socially, both in space and in time. Indeed the first two centuries of printing from movable types were motivated much more by the desire to see ancient and medieval books than by the need to read and write new ones. Until 1700 much more than 50 per cent of all printed books were ancient or medieval. Not only antiquity but also the Middle Ages were given to the first reading public of the printed word. And the medieval texts were by far the most popular.

Like any other extension of man, typography had psychic and social consequences that suddenly shifted previous boundaries and

"The Printed Word: Architect of Nationalism." From Marshall McLuhan, *Understanding Media: The Extensions of Man* (New York: McGraw-Hill Book Company, 1964), hardcover ed., pp. 170–78. Copyright © 1964 by Marshall McLuhan. Used with permission of McGraw-Hill Book Company and Routledge & Kegan Paul Ltd.

patterns of culture. In bringing the ancient and medieval worlds into fusion—or, as some would say, confusion—the printed book created a third world, the modern world, which now encounters a new electric technology or a new extension of man. Electric means of moving of information are altering our typographic culture as sharply as print modified medieval manuscript and scholastic culture.

Beatrice Warde has recently described in *Alphabet* an electric display of letters painted by light. It was a Norman McLaren movie advertisement of which she asks

> Do you wonder that I was late for the theatre that night, when I tell you that I saw two club-footed Egyptian A's . . . walking off arm-in-arm with the unmistakable swagger of a music-hall comedy-team? I saw base-serifs pulled together as if by ballet shoes, so that the letters tripped off literally *sur les pointes* . . . after forty centuries of the *necessarily static* Alphabet, I saw what its members could do in the fourth dimension of Time, "flux," movement. You may well say that I was electrified.

Nothing could be farther from typographic culture with its "place for everything and everything in its place."

Mrs. Warde has spent her life in the study of typography and she shows sure tact in her startled response to letters that are not printed by types but painted by light. It may be that the explosion that began with phonetic letters (the "dragon's teeth" sowed by King Cadmus) will reverse into "implosion" under the impulse of the instant speed of electricity. The alphabet (and its extension into typography) made possible the spread of the power that is knowledge, and shattered the bonds of tribal man, thus exploding him into agglomeration of individuals. Electric writing and speed pour upon him, instantaneously and continuously, the concerns of all other men. He becomes tribal once more. The human family becomes one tribe again.

Any student of the social history of the printed book is likely to be puzzled by the lack of understanding of the psychic and social effects of printing. In five centuries explicit comment and awareness of the effects of print on human sensibility are very scarce. But the same observation can be made about all the extensions of man, whether it be clothing or the computer. An extension appears to be an amplification of an organ, a sense or a function, that inspires the central nervous system to a self-protective gesture of numbing of the extended area, at least so far as direct inspection and awareness are concerned. Indirect comment on the effects of the printed book is available in abundance in the work of Rabelais, Cervantes, Montaigne, Swift, Pope, and Joyce. They used typography to create new art forms.

Psychically the printed book, an extension of the visual faculty, intensified perspective and the fixed point of view. Associated with the visual stress on point of view and the vanishing point that provides the illusion of perspective there comes another illusion that space is visual, uniform and continuous. The linearity precision and, uniformity of the arrangement of movable types are inseparable from these great cultural forms and innovations of Renaissance experience. The new intensity of visual stress and private point of view in the first century of printing were united to the means of self-expression made possible by the typographic extension of man.

Socially, the typographic extension of man brought in nationalism, industrialism, mass markets, and universal literacy and education. For print presented an image of repeatable precision that inspired totally new forms of extending social energies. Print released great psychic and social energies in the Renaissance, as today in Japan or Russia, by breaking the individual out of the traditional group while providing a model of how to add individual to individual in massive agglomeration of power. The same spirit of private enterprise that emboldened authors and artists to cultivate self-expression led other men to create giant corporations, both military and commercial.

Perhaps the most significant of the gifts of typography to man is that of detachment and noninvolvement—the power to act without reacting. Science since the Renaissance has exalted this gift which has become an embarrassment in the electric age, in which all people are involved in all others at all times. The very word "disinterested," expressing the loftiest detachment and ethical integrity of typographic man, has in the past decade been increasingly used to mean: "He couldn't care less." The same integrity indicated by the term "disinterested" as a mark of the scientific and scholarly temper of a literate and enlightened society is now increasingly repudiated as "specialization" and fragmentation of knowledge and sensibility. The fragmenting and analytic power of the printed word in our psychic lives gave us that "dissociation of sensibility" which in the arts and literature since Cézanne and since Baudelaire has been a top priority for elimination in every program of reform in taste and knowledge. In the "implosion" of the electric age the separation of thought and feeling has come to seem as strange as the departmentalization of knowledge in schools and universities. Yet it was precisely the power to separate thought and feeling, to be able to act without reacting, that split literate man out of the tribal world of close family bonds in private and social life.

Typography was no more an addition to the scribal art than the motorcar was an addition to the horse. Printing had its "horseless carriage" phase of being misconceived and misapplied during its first decades, when it was not uncommon for the purchaser of a printed book to take it to a scribe to have it copied and illustrated. Even in the early eighteenth century a "textbook" was still defined as a "Classick Author written very wide by the Students, to give room for an Interpretation dictated by the Master, &c., to be inserted in the Interlines" (O.E.D.). Before printing, much of the time in school and college classrooms was spent in making such texts. The classroom tended to be a *scriptorium* with a commentary. The student was an editor-publisher. By the same token the book market was a second-hand market of relatively scarce items. Printing changed learning and marketing processes alike. The book was the first teaching machine and also the first mass-produced commodity. In amplifying and extending the written word, typography revealed and greatly extended the structure of writing. Today, with the cinema and the electric speed-up of information movement, the formal structure of the printed word, as of mechanism in general, stands forth like a branch washed up on the beach. A new medium is never an addition to an old one, nor does it leave the old one in peace. It never ceases to oppress the older media until it finds new shapes and positions for them. Manuscript culture had sustained an oral procedure in education that was called "scholasticism" at its higher levels; but by putting the same text in front of any given number of students or readers print ended the scholastic regime of oral disputation very quickly. Print provided a vast new memory for past writings that made a personal memory inadequate.

Margaret Mead has reported that when she brought several copies of the same book to a Pacific island there was great excitement. The natives had seen books, but only one copy of each, which they had assumed to be unique. Their astonishment at the identical character of several books was a natural response to what is after all the most magical and potent aspect of print and mass production. It involves a principle of extension by homogenization that is the key to understanding Western power. The open society is open by virtue of a uniform typographic educational processing that permits indefinite expansion of any group by additive means. The printed book based on typographic uniformity and repeatability in the visual order was the first teaching machine, just as typography was the first mechanization of a handicraft. Yet is spite of the extreme fragmentation or specialization of human action necessary to achieve the printed word, the printed book represents a rich composite of previous cultural inventions. The total effort embodied in the illustrated book in print offers a striking example of the variety of separate acts of invention that are requisite to bring about a new technological result.

The psychic and social consequences of print included an extension of its fissile and uniform character to the gradual homogenization of diverse regions with the resulting amplification of power, energy, and aggression that we associate with new nationalisms. Psychically, the visual extension and amplification of the individual by print had many effects. Perhaps as striking as any other is the one mentioned by Mr. E. M. Forster, who, when discussing some Renaissance types, suggested that "the printing press, then only a century old, had been mistaken for an engine of immortality, and men had hastened to commit to it deeds and passions for the benefit of future ages." People began to act as though immortality were inherent in the magic repeatability and extensions of print.

Another significant aspect of the uniformity and repeatability of the printed page was the pressure it exerted toward "correct" spelling, syntax, and pronunciation. Even more notable were the effects of print in separating poetry from song, and prose from oratory, and popular from educated speech. In the matter of poetry it turned out that, as poetry could be read without being heard, musical instruments could also be played without accompanying any verses. Music veered from the spoken word, to converge again with Bartók and Schoenberg.

With typography the process of separation (or explosion) of functions went on swiftly at all levels and in all spheres; nowhere was this matter observed and commented on with more bitterness than in the plays of Shakespeare. Especially in *King Lear,* Shakespeare provided an image or model of the process of quantification and fragmentation as it entered the world of politics and of family life. Lear at the very opening of the play presents "our darker purpose" as a plan of delegation of powers and duties:

> Only we shall retain
> The name, and all th' addition to a King;
> The sway, revenue, execution of the rest,
> Beloved sons, be yours: which to confirm,
> This coronet part between you.

This act of fragmentation and delegation blasts Lear, his kingdom, and his family. Yet to divide and rule was the dominant new idea of the organization of power in the Renaissance. "Our darker purpose" refers to Machiavelli himself, who had developed an individualist and quantitative idea of power that struck more fear in that time than

Marx in ours. Print, then, challenged the corporate patterns of medieval organization as much as electricity now challenges our fragmented individualism.

The uniformity and repeatability of print permeated the Renaissance with the idea of time and space as continuous measurable quan-
tities. The immediate effect of this idea was to desacralize the world
of nature and the world of power alike. The new technique of control of physical processes by segmentation and fragmentation separated God and Nature as much as Man and Nature, or man and man.
Shock at this departure from traditional vision and inclusive awareness was often directed toward the figure of Machiavelli, who had
merely spelled out the new quantitative and neutral or scientific ideas
of force as applied to the manipulation of kingdoms.

Shakespeare's entire work is taken up with the themes of the
new delimitations of power, both kingly and private. No greater
horror could be imagined in his time than the spectacle of Richard
II, the sacral king, undergoing the indignities of imprisonment and
denudation of his sacred prerogatives. It is in *Troilus and Cressida,*
however, that the new cults of fissile, irresponsible power, public and
private, are paraded as a cynical charade of atomistic competition:

> Take the instant way;
> For honour travels in a strait so narrow
> Where one but goes abreast: keep, then, the path;
> For emulation hath a thousand sons
> That one by one pursue: if you give way,
> Or hedge aside from the direct forthright,
> Like to an enter'd tide they all rush by
> And leave you hindmost . . .
>
> (III, iii)

The image of society as segmented into a homogeneous mass of quan-
tified appetites shadows Shakespeare's vision in the later plays.

Of the many unforeseen consequences of typography, the emergence of nationalism is, perhaps, the most familiar. Political unification of populations by means of vernacular and language groupings was unthinkable before printing turned each vernacular into an
extensive mass medium. The tribe, an extended form of a family
of blood relatives, is exploded by print, and is replaced by an association of men homogeneously trained to be individuals. Nationalism
itself came as an intense new visual image of group destiny and
status, and depended on a speed of information movement unknown
before printing. Today nationalism as an image still depends on the
press but has all the electric media against it. In business, as in poli-

tics, the effect of even jet-plane speeds is to render the older national groupings of social organization quite unworkable. In the Renaissance it was the speed of print and the ensuing market and commercial developments that made nationalism (which is continuity and competition in homogeneous space) as natural as it was new. By the same token, the heterogeneities and noncompetitive discontinuities of medieval guilds and family organization had become a great nuisance as speed-up of information by print called for more fragmentation and uniformity of function. The Benvenuto Cellinis, the goldsmith-cum-painter-cum-sculptor-cum-writer-cum-condottiere, became obsolete.

Once a new technology comes into a social milieu it cannot cease to permeate that milieu until every institution is saturated. Typography has permeated every phase of the arts and sciences in the past five hundred years. It would be easy to document the processes by which the principles of continuity, uniformity, and repeatability have become the basis of calculus and of marketing, as of industrial production, entertainment, and science. It will be enough to point out that repeatability conferred on the printed book the strangely novel character of a uniformly priced commodity opening the door to price systems. The printed book had in addition the quality of portability and accessibility that had been lacking in the manuscript.

Directly associated with these expansive qualities was the revolution in expression. Under manuscript conditions the role of being an author was a vague and uncertain one, like that of a minstrel. Hence, self-expression was of little interest. Typography, however, created a medium in which it was possible to speak out loud and bold to the world itself, just as it was possible to circumnavigate the world of books previously locked up in a pluralistic world of monastic cells. Boldness of type created boldness of expression.

Uniformity reached also into areas of speech and writing, leading to a single tone and attitude to reader and subject spread throughout an entire composition. The "man of letters" was born. Extended to the spoken word, this literate *equitone* enabled literate people to maintain a single "high tone" in discourse that was quite devastating, and enabled nineteenth-century prose writers to assume moral qualities that few would now care to simulate. Permeation of the colloquial language with literate uniform qualities has flattened out educated speech till it is a very reasonable acoustic facsimile of the uniform and continuous visual effects of typography. From this technological effect follows the further fact that the humor, slang, and dramatic vigor of American-English speech are monopolies of the semi-literate.

These typographical matters for many people are charged with controversial values. Yet in any approach to understanding print it is necessary to stand aside from the form in question if its typical pressure and life are to be observed. Those who panic now about the threat of the newer media and about the revolution we are forging, vaster in scope than that of Gutenberg, are obviously lacking in cool visual detachment and gratitude for that most potent gift bestowed on Western man by literacy and typography: his power to act without reaction or involvement. It is this kind of specialization by dissociation that has created Western power and efficiency. Without this dissociation of action from feeling and emotion people are hampered and hesitant. Print taught men to say, "Damn the torpedoes. Full steam ahead!"

Chapter 4

literacy
and the non-literate
in Ghana

Jack Goody

It is a mistake to think of precolonial Africa as the dark continent unenlightened by the lamp of literacy. We do not, it is true, know of any early systems of writing which developed there, though some, such as the famous Vai, and the lesser known scripts, such as Nsibidi, were invented after the colonial period had begun. But alphabetic writing of Middle Eastern origin made its mark outside Egypt as Judaism, then Christianity, and finally Islam penetrated into the northern sectors of the continent. Christianity and its literature continued to be important in Ethiopia, and Islam spread in the savannah country of the West and along the coastal regions of East Africa, bringing its teachers, its brotherhoods, its books.

The nature of religious literacy inevitably placed certain limitations on its effectiveness; it was a restricted literacy both in terms of the proportion who could read and the uses to which writing was put. Moreover, its religious basis meant that a major function was communication to or about God. While courts utilized writing for a number of purposes—historical, treaty-making, epistolary—it was the magical-religious aspect which most impressed the majority of the population. They were concerned with writing as a means of communicating with God and other supernatural agencies, rather than as a means of social and personal advancement. Certainly there was nothing to be ashamed of in being non-literate.

But the position is now changing. The new literacy, associated with predominantly secular teachings at European-type schools, lies at

"Literacy and the Non-Literate in Ghana" (editor's title). From Jack Goody, "Literacy and the Non-Literate," *Times Literary Supplement* (London), May 12, 1972, pp. 539–40. Reprinted by permission of the author.

the basis of a dual economy, a dual economy of the spirit as well as of labour. What does the advent of modern literacy do to societies that were previously non-literate? The extent to which new commercial and political activities depend upon literacy hardly needs stressing. The growth of towns, the growth of the economy, the growth of the political system involving mass participation, the growth of the media: all these depend to a greater or lesser extent upon changes in the system of communications. But 80 percent of Africa, as of other parts of the developing world, remains rural. What effect does the growth of literacy in their midst have on this segment of the population?

It gives rise at once to an extending ladder of mobility. It forces the gaze towards considerations of achievement rather than birth. This criterion may not be universally applied, but it is always relevant. In Africa the result has been a drastic modification of existing elites. Some of the slaves sent to school, when their owners wished to avoid the District Commissioner's pressure to recruit their own sons, have achieved more than members of the ruling lineage. Frailty paid off. The first literate has become the first M.P. for his district. This new system of achievement carries a new system of rewards leading to a new system of stratification. It takes the successful individual out of the local setting and enables him to operate on a national level; it enables him to command national or even international salaries. The new elite, seeking to maintain its own position, encourages its children to pursue the same goals, and the system of education, earlier an open channel to social mobility, now becomes the instrument of status preservation.

But even in the early phase it is not simply a matter of achievement; there is also a yawning gap between those who have been to school and those who have not, between haves and have nots. For the non-literate, social change is associated with "knowing book." In David Rubadiri's novel, *No Bride Price*, the hero Lombe goes to his natal village and is visited by his uncle.

> He was an old man who had seen life. In his village he had prepared himself to live a full life. But the change came. It was not a sudden change. A white man with a book in his hand. Every evening this white man with the book had sat at the edge of the village and played with the children.

Under these conditions there is inevitably a sense of inferiority which forces the pace of educational development, thus leading to an over-development of schools. For there are soon too many educated for the available jobs. While people have been educated out of subsistence agriculture (as they see it), there is no alternative occupation. We find the classic dichotomy, typical of Ceylon, of Egypt and becoming more typical of Africa: the educated unemployed, the school leaver who refuses to go back on the land, who regards himself as destined for a white-collar job.

Thus, in many parts of the continent the effect of introducing literacy is, temporarily at least, to split the population into two halves, one of which is largely rural, the other mainly urban. The split may not always take the form of a physical separation. But many of the literates working in the country will be doing so reluctantly, with their eyes on the town and on its life. For literacy achieved through formal education is the main method of self-advancement, of reaching beyond the level of subsistence farming. Indeed it is not only at the subsistence level that agriculture is considered to provide an inadequate life; the stress of school-learnt values falls elsewhere, in favour of white-collar jobs (or "white-colour" jobs, as they are sometimes called in West Africa), preferably in an urban setting.

Let us look at the situation in Northern Ghana in greater depth. Writing was not unknown in this region before the colonial conquest. Indeed that conquest was recorded by a Muslim author, Al-Hajj Umar of Salaga, who wrote a widely distributed poem on the coming of the Christians. In B. G. Martin's translation, it runs:

> A sun of disaster has risen in the West,
> Glaring down on people and populated places . . .
> The Christian calamity has come upon us
> Like a dust-cloud.
> At the start of the affair, they came
> Peacefully,
> With soft sweet talk.
> "We've come to trade," they said,
> "To reform the beliefs of the people,
> To halt oppression here below, and theft,
> To clean up and overthrow corruption."
> Not all of us grasped their motives,
> So now we've become their inferiors.
> They deluded us with little gifts
> And fed us with tasty foods . . .
> But recently they've changed their tune.

Literacy was used by Muslims for a variety of purposes, principally religious ones. But the rulers were rarely if ever literate. They used some literates as scribes and secretaries but, unlike the later Fulani conquerors of Northern Nigeria, they did not themselves know how to read and write; and indeed knowledge of these skills was seen as inimical to the practice of war and government. In this respect the situation was similar to certain kingdoms in the ancient Middle East, where rulers were not necessarily literate and where those who could write might have a status inferior to those who could not. Indeed, the word scribe has something of a pejorative implication to this day: a menial intellectual, at hand for the purposes of administering to the ruling class.

With the advent of colonial rule, the situation changed; the value of literacy as a means of social and personal advancement was immediately clear. The new conquerors used writing at every stage in their administration of the country; once they had locked away the Maxim guns in their armoury, it was the pen and telegraph that took over. The increasing dependence on written communication manifested itself not only internally, but also in communications with the subject peoples. These had to be trained to man the burgeoning bureaucracy and to extend this communication to the people themselves. In Northern Ghana the first schools were established by the army and by an intrusive mission. More informal instruction was arranged in the remote areas. The D.C. of Lawra established a "Hausa" school for the sons of headmen, who were to act as messengers between district headquarters and their father's villages. With the introduction of the system of Native Authorities in 1932, chiefs had their own clerks, with their own bureaucracies. And later still, pressure was exerted for chiefs themselves to be literate, so that they could participate in the full gamut of council activities, agenda, minutes, memoranda and returns.

Though it was an advantage for chiefs to be literates, for members of parliament, first elected in 1951, there was no alternative. Consequently it was the school teachers and the clerks who were the obvious candidates for these offices, which turned out to be of such high status in the community. Not only did they command a salary which was initially made comparable to that of a British M.P. (and hence vastly in excess of their previous earnings, or indeed of what they were likely to get if they were not re-elected), but there were abundant opportunities for doing favours and receiving rewards. By local standards, M.P.'s did immensely well and by 1966 theirs was often the most substantial house in the locality, though some officials such as the D.C. and the Clerk to the Council were beginning to catch up.

All this mobility had been made possible by literacy, by education. Indeed the effects are so dominating that a two-sector economy, trained partly in school, partly in the home, however desirable from the economic standpoint in phasing in the new developments, in maintaining a balance in educational investment, in keeping going the production of food, becomes virtually impossible to accept as part of a deliberate national plan. As citizens, the non-literate population would be excluded from so much, at least on the political level. They cannot read, much less understand, the law; appearing in front of a magistrate or judge, they are offered a book or a "fetish" on which to swear; acceptance of the latter identifies them as inferior, as illiterate, as "pagan." When they receive a letter from a son working elsewhere as a labourer, they have to find, and probably reward, a literate to read it. If they want to reply, they may have to approach one of the letter-writers sitting outside the local post-office. When the newspapers arrive, they are again left out. Though in recent years the transistor radio has done something to lessen the divide, it can never bridge it altogether. When the tax-man comes, he can cheat them with the receipt. Even the new religions are written, the priests literate, propagating the knowledge of the Book, which contains the secrets of life and death. They are at the mercy of a hostile world, geared to the man who can read and write. That is what development, modernization, independence, is all about.

Yet the world of the non-literate is not dead. His culture continues in a modified form and even finds some favour among the new elite. And there is evidence too of some counter-action. In Northern Ghana there have been signs if not of a parents' strike, at least of increasing reluctance to send children to school. Despite the avenues that have been opened up for the successfully literate, the standards of education required for new posts are constantly rising as the output of secondary school, technical college and university increases. With a limited number of jobs available for those who do not go to secondary school, the boy finds himself having to scrape a living loading lorries or running messages. Meanwhile he himself is unwilling to return to the farm. Seeing this happen more and more, and seeing too the lack of help given by educated sons to their old or infirm parents, people in some areas are becoming increasingly reluctant to send their children to school; not only do schoolboys fail to contribute to their own livelihood, they fail to help later on, especially if they are unemployed. The consequence has been the closure of a number of rural schools.

How does the advent of literacy affect the quality of life at the village level? One general feature of writing dominates the process of its introduction into non-literate societies: its ability to preserve speech so that communication can take place over space and over time. It is a process of distancing, which affects the personal as well as the national level.

The way it does so can be seen from a community in Northern Ghana. The village of Birifu had had a primary school for some twenty years when I returned there in 1971. Not one of its scholars has remained in the village; all left to get employment elsewhere. How did writing affect those that stayed? Clearly, it introduced a radical division between those who "knew book" and those who did not. The literate returned to the village occasionally, for funerals or for other celebrations, but he was not concerned with its day-to-day functioning. At Christmas there was a great exodus from the towns, and over the official holiday many literates returned to their natal villages, took part in settling some disputes and provoking others, and held meetings of "The Young Men's Society" which only they were allowed to join. For this purpose, they elected a chairman, treasurer and secretary whose first duty was to keep a written record. In this way, decisions are formalized, made permanent and thus less easy to change.

Because the literates came and went like flocks of migrating birds, they made little direct impact on village life. Yet the presence of schoolboys was nevertheless making a mark. At each funeral, food, drink and money pass between the bereaved and their relatives in a complicated series of transactions. Each is reciprocal, in that it has to be acknowledged immediately and repaid eventually—at a corresponding occasion. The concern of people to keep track of these transfers of property shows itself in the fact that today one often sees schoolboys keeping a record of what has been handed over. Among labour migrants in a town in Southern Ghana, one investigator often found himself called upon to write down the income and the outgoings at similar ceremonies. For the absence of writing places a restriction on the number of such items the average man can recall as well as the length of time he can retain the information. Many women who provide drinks or cooked food for salaried workers allow credit by the month. When payday comes at the end of that period, they can be seen gathering around the workshop gates waiting for settlement. But the number of customers and hence their rate of profit is limited by their memory.

Liberation from these restrictions on the efficiency of the memory store comes with pencil and paper. Even a very limited knowledge of writing can be of help to a cook making out a shopping list or a market mammy keeping a record of the credit offered. It is just this need for elementary accounting that marks the early use of writing in Babylonia, Egypt and early Greece (Linear B). This elementary computation was a precursor of the flowering of book-keeping in the Italian Renaissance, and its development by the burghers of Western Europe, where painters like Rembrandt pictured the literate merchants poring over their double-entry account books.

In Southern Ghana, the recording of funeral contributions has been even further formalized by an enterprising printer who has produced books of receipts in triplicate for just such an occasion. One fills in the form (of which a specimen is reproduced below), tears out a sheet, and dispatches the coloured piece of paper to the home of the donor by the hand of a small boy.

The format requires a word of explanation. It is an acknowledgment by the bereaved of a monetary contribution to the expenses of

---

Thanks For Sympathy

....19.........

We acknowledge with thanks the receipt of your kind donation

of... New Cedis

....New Pesewas

From...

To...

In the event of our failure to meet you tomorrow or the day after, we beg you to accept our sincere thanks for your kind Donation & attendance

N₵...

....
RECEIVER

---

a funeral. Thanks are not normally given at the time of the ceremony itself but at a subsequent visit to the giver, which is known as "greeting." The sentence at the foot of the form (above the legitimating signature) is a prepacked apology for the absence of a face-to-face encounter. It is a written substitute for oral contact, like the visitors' book of the former colonial Commissioner which still stands in a sentry box outside the Residency of the Chief Regional Office in Tamale, the capital of the Northern Region of Ghana, or like the visiting card left at the house of a newly-arrived neighbour.

We are witnessing here a process of distancing, of depersonalizing, social contacts. Indeed, in the spatially mobile situation in which they live, with not only the educated but also labourers travelling from less to more developed areas to sell their services, social relationships inevitably get dispersed widely over the ground and writing becomes the main means by which people can keep in touch. Nevertheless, when communication can be reduced to a few marks on a piece of paper rather than take place in the more concrete ambience of the face-to-face situation, the quality of interpersonal relationships is inevitably thinned; the multiplex relations of the village give way to single-stranded contacts that are more functionally specific, more manipulable, more "impersonal."

The change in the quality of life is inevitable; the rural community is no longer the centre of the world even for the majority of those who were born there, though it still retains an important place in the lives of all of them. The advent of literacy is perhaps the single most important factor in the changing situation, though in Birifu its visible influence on the village is limited, since all literates migrate. Perhaps its most radical effect on those who remain behind is that they begin to see themselves as inferior to those who have learnt book and gone away. Whereas formerly it was the migrant who lost contact with the centre of his world, now he gains by going. Exile is a desirable end. And while literacy was valued in the past even among the non-literate peoples, writing was always an auxiliary mode of communication. More important was the visit, the audience, the discussion, the palaver, where one went into the presence of one's chief or one's peers. Even in the Muslim areas, writing was but one specialization among many. Now literacy dominates the wider social system; the non-literate of yesterday has become the illiterate of today.

Chapter 5

literate culture:
some general considerations

Jack Goody and Ian Watt

It is hardly possible, in this brief survey, to determine what importance must be attributed to the alphabet as the cause or as the necessary condition of the seminal intellectual innovations that occurred in the Greek world during the centuries that followed the diffusion of writing; nor, indeed, does the nature of the evidence give much ground for believing that the problem can ever be fully resolved. The present argument must, therefore, confine itself to suggesting that some crucial features of Western culture came into being in Greece soon after the existence, for the first time, of a rich urban society in which a substantial portion of the population was able to read and write; and that, consequently, the overwhelming debt of the whole of contemporary civilization to classical Greece must be regarded as in some measure the result, not so much of the Greek genius, as of the intrinsic differences between non-literate (or protoliterate) and literate societies— the latter being mainly represented by those societies using the Greek alphabet and its derivatives. If this is so, it may help us to take our contrast between the transmission of the cultural heritage in non-literate and alphabetically literate societies a little further.

To begin with, the ease of alphabetic reading and writing was probably an important consideration in the development of political democracy in Greece; in the fifth century a majority of the free citizens could apparently read the laws, and take an active part in elections and legislation. Democracy as we know it, then, is from the beginning

"Literate Culture: Some General Considerations," by Jack Goody and Ian Watt. From Jack Goody, ed., *Literacy in Traditional Societies* (New York: Cambridge University Press, 1968), pp. 55–63. (Most footnotes have been deleted.) Reprinted by permission of Cambridge University Press. This essay was first published in 1963.

associated with widespread literacy; and so to a large extent is the notion of the world of knowledge as transcending political units; in the Hellenic world diverse people and countries were given a common administrative system and a unifying cultural heritage through the written word. Greece is therefore considerably closer to being a model for the world-wide intellectual tradition of the contemporary literate world than those earlier civilizations of the Orient which each had its own localized traditions of knowledge: as Oswald Spengler put it, "*Writing is the grand symbol of the Far.*" [1]

Yet although the idea of intellectual, and to some extent political, universalism is historically and substantively linked with literate culture, we too easily forget that this brings with it other features which have quite different implications, and which go some way to explain why the long-cherished and theoretically feasible dream of an "educated democracy" and a truly egalitarian society has never been realized in practice. One of the basic premises of liberal reform over the last century and a half has been that of James Mill, as it is described in the *Autobiography* of his son, John Stuart Mill:

> So complete was my father's reliance on the influence of reason over the minds of mankind, whenever it is allowed to reach them, that he felt as if all would be gained if the whole population were taught to read, if all sorts of opinions were allowed to be addressed to them by word and in writing, and if, by means of the suffrage, they could nominate a legislature to give effect to the opinions they adopted [p. 74].

All these things have been accomplished since the days of the Mills, but nevertheless "all" has not been "gained"; and some causes of this shortfall may be found in the intrinsic effects of literacy on the transmission of the cultural heritage, effects which can be seen most clearly by contrasting them with their analogues in non-literate society.

The writing down of some of the main elements in the cultural tradition in Greece, we say, brought about an awareness of two things: of the past as different from the present; and of the inherent inconsistencies in the picture of life as it was inherited by the individual from the cultural tradition in its recorded form. These two effects of widespread alphabetic writing, it may be surmised, have continued and multiplied themselves ever since, and at an increasing pace since the development of printing. "The printers," Jefferson remarked, "can never leave us in a state of perfect rest and union of opinion," and as book follows book and newspaper newspaper, the notion of rational

---

[1] [In 1968 Goody wrote that he and Watt "gave less explicit credit to the potentialities of non-phonetic writing than is deserved." See his comments on pp. 20–24 of *Literacy in Traditional Societies.*—Ed.]

agreement and democratic coherence among men has receded further and further away, while Plato's attacks on the venal purveyors of knowledge in the market-place have gained increased relevance.

But the inconsistency of the totality of written expression is perhaps less striking than its enormous bulk and its vast historical depth. Both of these have always seemed insuperable obstacles to those seeking to reconstruct society on a more unified and disciplined model: we find the objection in the book-burners of all periods; and it appears in many more respectable thinkers. In Jonathan Swift, for example, whose perfectly rational Houyhnhnms "have no letters," and whose knowledge "consequently . . . is all traditional." These oral traditions were of a scale, Swift tells us, that enabled "the historical part" to be "easily preserved without burthening their memories." Not so with the literate tradition, for, lacking the resources of unconscious adaptation and omission which exist in the oral transmission, the cultural repertoire can only grow; there are more words than anybody knows the meaning of—some 142,000 vocabulary entries in a college dictionary like the *Webster's New World*. This unlimited proliferation also characterizes the written tradition in general: the mere size of the literate repertoire means that the proportion of the whole which any one individual knows must be infinitesimal in comparison with what obtains in oral culture. Literate society, merely by having no system of elimination, no "structural amnesia," prevents the individual from participating fully in the total cultural tradition to anything like the extent possible in non-literate society.

One way of looking at this lack of any literate equivalent to the homeostatic organization of the cultural tradition in non-literate society is to see literate society as inevitably committed to an ever-increasing series of culture lags. The content of the cultural tradition grows continually, and in so far as it affects any particular individual he becomes a palimpsest composed of layers of beliefs and attitudes belonging to different stages in historical time. So too, eventually, does society at large, since there is a tendency for each social group to be particularly influenced by systems of ideas belonging to different periods in the nation's development; both to the individual, and to the groups constituting society, the past may mean very different things.

From the standpoint of the individual intellectual, of the literate specialist, the vista of endless choices and discoveries offered by so extensive a past can be a source of great stimulation and interest; but when we consider the social effects of such an orientation, it becomes apparent that the situation fosters the alienation that has characterized so many writers and philosophers of the West since the last century. It was surely, for example, this lack of social amnesia in alphabetic cultures which led Nietzsche to describe "we moderns" as "wandering encyclopaedias," unable to live and act in the present and obsessed by a " 'historical sense' that injures and finally destroys the living thing, be it a man or a people or a system of culture." Even if we dismiss Nietzsche's views as extreme, it is still evident that the literate individual has in practice so large a field of personal selection from the total cultural repertoire that the odds are strongly against his experiencing the cultural tradition as any sort of patterned whole.

From the point of view of society at large, the enormous complexity and variety of the cultural repertoire obviously creates problems of an unprecedented order of magnitude. It means, for example, that since Western literate societies are characterized by these always increasing layers of cultural tradition, they are incessantly exposed to a more complex version of the kind of culture conflict that has been held to produce *anomie* in oral societies when they come into contact with European civilization, changes which, for example, have been illustrated with a wealth of absorbing detail by Robert Redfield in his studies of Central America.

Another important consequence of alphabetic culture relates to social stratification. In the protoliterate cultures, with their relatively difficult non-alphabetic systems of writing, there existed a strong barrier between the writers and the non-writers; but although the "democratic" scripts made it possible to break down this particular barrier, they led eventually to a vast proliferation of more or less tangible distinctions based on what people had read. Achievement in handling the tools of reading and writing is obviously one of the most important axes of social differentiation in modern societies; and this differentiation extends on to more minute differences between professional specializations so that even members of the same socio-economic groups of literate specialists may hold little intellectual ground in common.

Nor, of course, are these variations in the degree of participation in the literate tradition, together with their effects on social structure, the only causes of tension. For, even within a literate culture, the oral tradition—the transmission of values and attitudes in face-to-face contact—nevertheless remains the primary mode of cultural orientation, and, to varying degrees, it is out of step with the various literate traditions. In some respects, perhaps, this is fortunate. The tendency of the modern mass-communications industries, for example, to promote ideals of conspicuous consumption which cannot be realized by more than a limited proportion of society might well have much more radical consequences but for the fact that each individual exposed to such pressures is also a member of one or more primary groups whose oral converse is probably much more realistic and conservative in its ideological tendency; the mass media are not the only, and they are probably not even the main, social influences on the contemporary cultural tradition as a whole.

Primary group values are probably even further removed from those of the "high" literate culture, except in the case of the literate specialists. This introduces another kind of culture conflict, and one which is of cardinal significance for Western civilization. If, for example, we return to the reasons for the relative failure of universal compulsory education to bring about the intellectual, social and political results that James Mill expected, we may well lay a major part of the blame on the gap between the public literate tradition of the school and the very different and indeed often directly contradictory private oral traditions of the pupil's family and peer group. The high degree of differentiation in exposure to the literate tradition sets up a basic division which cannot exist in non-literate society: the division between the various shades of literacy and illiteracy. This conflict, of course, is most dramatically focused in the school, the key institution of society. As Margaret Mead has pointed out: "Primitive education was a process by which continuity was maintained between parents and children. . . . Modern education includes a heavy emphasis upon the function of education to create discontinuities—to turn the child . . . of the illiterate into the literate." A similar and probably even more acute stress develops in many cases between the school and the peer group; and, quite apart from the difficulties arising from the substantive differences between the two orientations, there seem to be factors in the very nature of literate methods which make them ill suited to bridge the gap between the street-corner society and the blackboard jungle.

First, because although the alphabet, printing, and universal free education have combined to make the literate culture freely available to all on a scale never previously approached, the literate mode of communication is such that it does not impose itself as forcefully or as uniformly as is the case with the oral transmission of the cultural tradition. In non-literate society every social situation cannot but bring the individual into contact with the group's patterns of thought, feeling and action: the choice is between the cultural tradition—or solitude. In a literate society, however, and quite apart from the difficulties arising from the scale and complexity of the "high" literate tradition, the mere fact that reading and writing are normally solitary activities means that in so far as the dominant cultural tradition is a literate one, it is very easy to avoid; as Bertha Phillpotts wrote in her study of Icelandic literature:

> Printing so obviously makes knowledge accessible to all that we are
> inclined to forget that it also makes knowledge very easy to avoid. . . .
> A shepherd in an Icelandic homestead, on the other hand, could not
> avoid spending his evenings in listening to the kind of literature which
> interested the farmer. The result was a degree of really national culture
> such as no nation of today has been able to achieve.

The literate culture, then, is much more easily avoided than the oral
one; and even when it is not avoided its actual effects may be relatively shallow. Not only because, as Plato argued, the effects of reading
are intrinsically less deep and permanent than those of oral converse;
but also because the abstractness of the syllogism and of the Aristotelian categorizations of knowledge do not correspond very directly with
common experience. The abstractness of the syllogism, for example,
of its very nature disregards the individual's social experience and
immediate personal context; and the compartmentalization of knowledge similarly restricts the kind of connections which the individual
can establish and ratify with the natural and social world. The essential way of thinking of the specialist in literate culture is funda-
mentally at odds with that of daily life and common experience; and
the conflict is embodied in the long tradition of jokes about absent-
minded professors.

It is, of course, true that contemporary education does not present problems exactly in the forms of Aristotelian logic and taxonomy;
but all our literate modes of thought have been profoundly influenced
by them. In this, perhaps, we can see a major difference, not only from
the transmission of the cultural heritage of oral societies, but from
those of protoliterate ones. Thus Marcel Granet relates the nature of
the Chinese writing system to the "concreteness" of Chinese thought,
and his picture of its primary concentration on social action and traditional norms suggests that the cultural effect of the writing system
was in the direction of intensifying the sort of homeostatic conserva-
tion found in non-literate cultures; it was indeed conceptualized in the
Confucian *tao-'tung*, or "orthodox transmission of the way." In this
connection it may be noted that the Chinese attitude to formal logic,
and to the categorization of knowledge in general, is an articulate expression of what happens in an oral culture. Mencius, for example,
speaks for the non-literate approach in general when he comments:
"Why I dislike holding to one point is that it injures the *tao*. It takes
up one point and disregards a hundred others."

The social tension between the oral and literate orientations in
Western society is, of course, complemented by an intellectual one. In
recent times the Englightenment's attack on myth as irrational super-
stition has often been replaced by a regressive yearning for some mod-

ern equivalent of the unifying function of myth: "Have not," W. B. Yeats asked, "all races had their first unity from a mythology that marries them to rock and hill?"

In this nostalgia for the world of myths Plato has had a long line of successors. The Rousseauist cult of the Noble Savage, for instance, paid unwitting tribute to the strength of the homogeneity of oral culture, to the yearning admiration of the educated for the peasant's simple but cohesive view of life, the timelessness of his living in the present, the unanalytic spontaneity that comes with an attitude to the world that is one of absorbed and uncritical participation, a participation in which the contradictions between history and legend, for example, or between experience and imagination, are not felt as problems. Such, for example, is the literary tradition of the European peasant from Cervantes' Sancho Panza to Tolstoy's Platon Karataev. Both are illiterate; both are rich in proverbial lore; both are untroubled by intellectual consistency; and both represent many of the values which, it was suggested above, are characteristic of oral culture. In these two works, *Don Quixote* and *War and Peace*, which might well be considered two of the supreme achievements of modern Western literature, an explicit contrast is made between the oral and literate elements of the cultural tradition. Don Quixote himself goes mad by reading books; while, opposed to the peasant Karataev, stands the figure of Pierre, an urban cosmopolitan, and a great reader. Tolstoy writes of Karataev that—in this like Mencius or like Malinowski's Trobrianders—he

> did not, and could not, understand the meaning of words apart from their context. Every word and every action of his was the manifestation of an activity unknown to him, which was his life. But his life, as he regarded it, had no meaning as a separate thing. It had a meaning only as part of a whole of which he was always conscious [*War and Peace*].

Tolstoy, of course, idealizes; but, conversely, even in his idealization he suggests one major emphasis of literate culture and one which we immediately associate with the Greeks—the stress upon the individual; Karataev does not regard "his life . . . as a separate thing." There are, of course, marked differences in the life histories of individual members of non-literate societies: the story of Crashing Thunder differs from that of other Winnebago; that of Baba of Karo from other Hausa women; and these differences are often given public recognition by ascribing to individuals a personal tutelary or guardian spirit. But on the whole there is less individualization of personal experience in oral cultures, which tend, in Durkheim's phrase, to be characterized by "mechanical solidarity"—by the ties between like persons,

rather than by a more complicated set of complementary relationships between individuals in a variety of roles. Like Durkheim, many
sociologists would relate this greater individualization of personal experience in literate societies to the effects of a more extensive division
of labour. There is no single explanation; but the techniques of reading and writing are undoubtedly of very great importance. There is,
first of all, the formal distinction which alphabetic culture has emphasized between the divine, the natural, and the human orders; secondly,
there is the social differentiation to which the institutions of literate
culture give rise; third, there is the effect of professional intellectual
specialization on an unprecedented scale; lastly, there is the immense
variety of choice offered by the whole corpus of recorded literature;
and from these four factors there ensues, in any individual case, the
highly complex totality deriving from the selection of these literate
orientations and from the series of primary groups in which the individual has also been involved.

As for personal awareness of this individualization, other factors
doubtless contributed, but writing itself (especially in its simpler, more
cursive forms) was of great importance. For writing, by objectifying
words, and by making them and their meaning available for much
more prolonged and intensive scrutiny than is possible orally, encourages private thought; the diary or the confession enables the individual to objectify his own experience, and gives him some check upon
the transmutations of memory under the influences of subsequent
events. And then, if the diary is later published, a wider audience can
have concrete experience of the differences that exist in the histories of
their fellow men from a record of a life which has been partially insu-
lated from the assimilative process of oral transmission.

The diary is, of course, an extreme case; but Plato's dialogues
themselves are evidence of the general tendency of writing to increase
the awareness of individual differences in behavior, and in the personality which lies behind them;[2] while the novel, which participates
in the autobiographical and confessional direction of such writers as
St. Augustine, Pepys and Rousseau, and purports to portray the inner
as well as the outer life of individuals in the real world, has replaced
the collective representations of myth and epic.

From the point of view of the general contrast between oral and
alphabetically literate culture, then, there is a certain identity between
the spirit of the Platonic dialogues and of the novel: both kinds of
writing express what is a characteristic intellectual effort of literate

    [2] In the *Theaetetus*, for example, emphasis is placed on the inner dialogue of
the soul in which it perceives ethical ideas "by comparing within herself things past
and present with the future" (186b).

culture, and present the process whereby the individual makes his own more or less conscious, more or less personal selection, rejection and accommodation among the conflicting ideas and attitudes in his culture. This general kinship between Plato and the characteristic art form of literate culture, the novel, suggests a further contrast between oral and literate societies: in contrast to the homeostatic transmission of the cultural tradition among non-literate peoples, literate society leaves more to its members; less homogeneous in its cultural tradition, it gives more free play to the individual, and particularly to the intellectual, the literate specialist himself; does so by sacrificing a single, ready-made orientation to life. And, in so far as an individual participates in the literate, as distinct from the oral, culture, such coherence as a person achieves is very largely the result of his personal selection, adjustment and elimination of items from a highly differentiated cultural repertoire; he is, of course, influenced by all the various social pressures, but they are so numerous that the pattern finally comes out as an individual one.

Much could be added by way of development and qualification on this point, as on much else that has been said above. The contrast could be extended, for example, by bringing it up to date and considering later developments in communication, from the invention of printing and of the power press to that of radio, cinema and television. All these latter, it may be surmised, derive much of their effectiveness as agencies of social orientation from the fact that their media do not have the abstract and solitary quality of reading and writing, but on the contrary share something of the nature and impact of the direct personal interaction which obtains in oral cultures. It may even be that these new modes of communicating sight and sound without any limit of time or place will lead to a new kind of culture: less inward and individualistic than literate culture, probably, and sharing some of the relative homogeneity, though not the mutuality, of oral society. . . .

PART TWO

the crisis
of
literacy

Section A

literacy, language, and politics

Contrary to popular belief, the crisis of language and literacy in the twentieth century is less a consequence of the electronic revolution than it is a symptom of the pervasive doubts about Western culture that emerged in response to the brutal facts of recent history.

In their efforts to account for the failures of Western institutions, many students of language, such as Douglas Bush, have linked the alleged corruption of language to the decline of humane culture and civilized politics.

That language of any kind is susceptible to "corruption" is, of course, an unprovable assertion—or, assuming corruptibility, that either political brutality or cultural demise is a necessary consequence. Too often those who have argued that we must maintain standards in grammar and usage have in reality been concerned more with maintaining class distinctions and cultural elitism than with demystifying the universe of discourse.

But even if it were possible to establish precise connections between language and politics, what could be done to enhance the vitality of language? Certainly it would be unwise to place much hope in the university, where for one hundred years freshmen have failed to learn much about language in the mandatory composition courses, and where some of the most cloying varieties of pseudoscientific jargon and prose styles have been born.

Not that English teachers don't try to find remedies for poor writing: each issue of *College English* brings a new solution to the problem of teaching English. But it is unlikely that any solution, no matter how brilliantly conceived, could purge the universe of discourse of the chaos inflicted on it by the vested interests of commerce, the military, and government. Their deadly rhetoric, as Herbert Marcuse shows in his essay, "The Closing of the Universe of Discourse,"

61

intentionally disrupts the processes of human communication in order to obtain selfish ends.

When everyone, or almost everyone, realizes these groups are in fact lying, yet continues to behave as though they were not, then the issue of literacy becomes vastly more complicated than problems of diction, syntax, and clarity of expression.

Unfortunately for the reader, Marcuse's opaque style demands considerable patience. But the brilliance of his analysis and the radical implications that flow from it are prerequisites for speculation about the future of literacy.

The crux of the problem is whether the vitality of language can be restored within, or in spite of, a framework of corrupting institutions. In *Speaking and Language,* Paul Goodman placed the reform of institutions above the reform of language:

> The forthright way to improve language is to improve the political and social institutions and the general moral culture. If there were different, and less, administration there would be less administrative double-talk. If people were more free and competent in their communities and jobs, they would be immune to demagogic rhetoric. If there were not so many ads, children would take words more seriously. If the children didn't go to school so much, some of them might learn to read English (p. 108).

Pending such developments, the writer must struggle to break free of "format" and find his own voice in living idiomatic speech.

Chapter 6

polluting our language

Douglas Bush

Along with our overriding anxieties about the state of the world and
our own country we are resentfully aware of shoddiness in cars, foods,
services, in almost everything except the language we use. While an
aroused public applauds the exposure of civic corruption and environmental pollution, neither the public at large nor officialdom has any
concern with the corruption and pollution of language except to contribute to it. And this kind of corruption is quite as disastrous as any
other, if not more so, partly because common violation of traditional
usage is an ugly debasement of our great heritage, partly because
sloppy English is a symptom and agent of sloppy thinking and feeling
and of sloppy communication and confusion. To the famous question,
"How do I know what I think till I hear what I say?" the answer
might be "Do you and I know then?"

The history of this relatively modern country has created problems that have not existed in the same way or degree in the older,
smaller, and much more cohesive European nations. In England the
South-East Midland dialect in which Chaucer wrote became standard
English, although down to our time other regional dialects have maintained an active nonstandard existence among the lower classes. But
in the United States obvious historical factors have worked against
such an accepted standard: the legacy of a frontier civilization, with
its individualistic indifference or hostility toward cultivated speech;
the relative absence of class distinctions (apart from those caused by
economic and hence educational disparities); the increasing intermix-

From Douglas Bush, "Polluting Our Language," *The American Scholar*, 41,
No. 2, Spring 1972, 238–47. Copyright © 1972 by the United Chapters of Phi Beta
Kappa. Reprinted by permission of the publishers.

ture of diverse races and nationalities; and so on. Thus, according to the irate linguist (or the lighthearted American librettist) of *My Fair Lady,* the French don't care what you do so long as you speak correctly, while in America English hasn't been spoken for years. At any rate we can see much recent evidence of the conspicuous spread of bad English; Gresham's law operates no less in the linguistic than in the monetary sphere. And it seems plain that among many writers, editors, publishers and printers there is growing indifference to the lowly but not insignificant matters of misspelling and misprints.

Whatever may be the case in other countries, in ours efforts to establish or reestablish serious respect for the mother tongue, for the precise use of words, for clarity, simplicity, and discriminating taste, have encountered much apathy or resistance, tacit or vocal, from average unconscious practice and, in recent decades, from very conscious academic doctrine. The only "errors" familiar to the mass of people seem to be the split infinitive and the ending of a sentence with a preposition, and neither of these usages is an error. As for academic doctrine, the publication in 1961 of the third edition of Webster brought on an immediate battle in which much ink and some blood were spilled. On one side were the makers and the defenders of the dictionary's widely permissive policy and procedure: the "standard" set up was current American speech; aiming at description, not prescription, the dictionary recorded, and by implication endorsed, all words, meanings and usages actually in use; it normally avoided invidious distinctions between "right" and "wrong." On such principles the idea of "error" has no validity: any intelligible expression that any people utter becomes automatically right and acceptable, no matter how it may violate orthodox rules of diction, grammar or idiom. Such wholesale pragmatism was decidedly a challenge, at least to those who believe that tennis requires a net. Along with much silent revulsion, a considerable number of writers, while recognizing the historical process of continuous change, reacted vehemently against a Philistine view of language based on the habits of the man in the street and insisted on traditional standards of language as molded by time and taste, by old writers and speakers as well as those of the moment. To such champions of good English the linguists replied with charges of pedantic schoolmarmishness, elitism, and the like.

That pitched battle died down, but people who have a conscience about language, who see the far-reaching consequences of linguistic corruption, have continued to express concern, because corruption continues to spread not merely in everyday speech and writing but in public utterances on war and peace, indeed in all areas and on all levels. A generation ago George Orwell emphasized the close connection between disorder in language and disorder in society (as, for instance, Roger Ascham, the Tudor humanist, and Milton had done in earlier ages). In an interview in the *New York Times* of October 19, 1971, W. H. Auden said: "As a poet—not as a citizen—there is only one political duty, and that is to defend one's language from corruption. And that is particularly serious now. It's being so quickly corrupted. When it's corrupted, people lose faith in what they hear, and this leads to violence." But such protests do not much affect the multitude, who need to be jolted out of their complacent insensitivity, a multitude that includes not only a large proportion of the upper middle class but persons of such exceptional intelligence and cultivation as writers and politicians.

To cite examples from these two elite groups, the front-page review in the *New York Times Book Review* of September 19, 1971, carried, as a boldface heading, a pronouncement on John Hawkes as "feasibly, our best writer"; a couple of months before that, Secretary of the Treasury John Connally, according to a highly reliable member of his audience, fervently proclaimed that "In the early sixties we were strong, we were virulent. . . ." These are only two recent reminders of the kind of English that has become increasingly common among the educated; such blunders, and countless others, would, we may believe, have been quite impossible a hundred years ago, when educated people were literate. During the past generation or two neither early teaching (often by doubtfully literate teachers) nor reading seems to have had much effect in holding back the tide of illiteracy. Very readable authorities on English and American usage, from the canonical Fowler to William Strunk and E. B. White, Theodore Bernstein and Wilson Follett, apparently are not read by the masses of people who need them; instead, these people, both upper and lower middle classes (if such terms may be used), create, absorb and propagate an ever-increasing body of what are no longer merely vulgar errors but constituent elements of American English. And American English, whatever its violations of established diction and idiom, always has chauvinistic force and heat behind it; many people would rather be wrong than be tainted with English English (not that contemporary English English is of flawless purity). Correctness smacks of effete gentility, which is abhorrent to American virility (or, to echo Secretary Connally, virulence). And recent American literature has yielded a notable flowering of the native tradition of toughness.

To intermix the concrete with the general, we might observe some random examples of the illiteracy that we meet on all sides, in print and on the air. It is more or less commonly accepted that there is such a word as "pablum," an item, if my memory serves, in Mr.

Agnew's copious vocabulary (I don't know how the Latin "pabulum" came to be both syncopated and domesticated); that "torturous" means "tortuous"; that "transpire" means "happen," "occur"; that "humanitarian" is the adjective corresponding to "the humanities"; that you "convince" someone to do something; that "otherwise" is an adjective (and that any noun may be converted into an adverb by the addition of "-wise"); that "reticent" means "reluctant" (for example, in a *New York Times* editorial of some years ago, "The commission's reticence to assess blame"); that "sensuous" means "sensual" and vice versa; that "fulsome" (that is, "grossly excessive") means something like "extremely good or favorable" ("The chairman gave a fulsome eulogy of the speaker"); that "connive" means "conspire"; that "hopefully" may be thrown into a sentence anywhere as a floating rib; that "media" and "data" are singular nouns; that the past tense of "fit" is "fit" (for example, *New Republic,* June 12, 1971, p. 36; August 7–14, p. 14). I might add a few examples, perhaps less common than those cited, which I have heard on the air: "The delegation's arrival was upheld by the weather"; "Two trustees escaped from prison last night"; and —on public TV—"I demure to that" (to render the commentator's pronunciation).

Wilson Follett affirmed that "affectation in an advanced culture is the chief agent of linguistic corruption." In regard to origins (or jargon, which will come up later) that may well be true, but the wholesale spread of corruption may surely be ascribed to mere infection, to the careless, unthinking assimilation of the floating germs that envelop us. The abolition, years ago, of "shall" (except for some freakish misuses) in favor of "will" as maid-of-all-work has wiped out the important distinction between simple futurity and determination ("I will not cease from mental fight, / Nor shall my sword sleep in my hand"). There is the ugly and almost universal use of "like" for "as" (legislative anxiety about cigarette advertising did not extend to cancerous grammar), and, in a lesser degree, the use of "as" for "like"— a reversal of accepted usage that has no warrant in ease, informality, or anything except perversity and contagion. Some indispensable words have been so thoroughly corrupted that they can no longer be used correctly without the probability of being misunderstood. A well-known American poet speaks of an artist's "flaunting of polite society"; a distinguished scholar-critic says that Milton "flaunts" botanical fact; the press secretary at the White House cannot think that the governor of Texas would "deliberately flaunt the wage-price freeze" (*New York Times,* August 20, 1971, p. 1). This misuse of "flaunt" for "flout" is of course sanctioned by Webster. Contrariwise, R. G. Martin's popular biography, *Jennie,* tells of "the flouting, fashionable beauties" of late Victorian times (vol. I, New York, 1969, p. 45). The use of "wrack" (wreck) in the sense of "rack" (torture) seems to be obliterating the right word. Bergen Evans, coauthor of *A Dictionary of Contemporary American Usage,* avows himself "wracked with admiration" for Theodore Bernstein, in a pamphlet issued by the publishers of Webster. The *New Republic* misfires in both words of a compound: "dissention-wracked" (December 11, 1971, p. 7). In the long catalogue of linguistic corruptions one of the most grievous— or, in the common phrase, "nerve-wracking"—is the case of "disinterested," which is almost always used in place of the now abandoned "uninterested." It is not clear why, since the usurper is not at all easier to utter than the right word; the result is that, as I said, one can't use "disinterested" correctly without the probability of being misunderstood—and there is no real synonym to fall back on.

All this adds up, not to greater force, enrichment and refinement, or clearer communication, but to the steady coarsening and blunting of the expressive and discriminating power of the language. For one thing, it threatens to cut us off from the great heritage that is a large part of what we possess. We can hardly echo Wordsworth's proud boast that we "speak the tongue / That Shakespeare spake," since we may before long lose the ability to read him; indeed many young people have lost it already. Perhaps, if the counterculture or subculture does not sweep away all literature but the immediately contemporary, a favorite comedy for schools will be abridged, rewritten in the language of the street, and rechristened *Like You Like It.* The sentiments I have been expressing are of course damned as old-fogeyish by progressive thinkers. Of the compilers of the third edition of Webster and their dropping of standard authors in favor of often insignificant contemporaries, Dwight Macdonald said: "They seem imperfectly aware of the fact that the past of a language is part of its present, that tradition is as much a fact as the violation of tradition." They seem also imperfectly aware that the use of language is, on varying levels of sophistication, an art (an unawareness shared by some modern and scholarly translators of the Bible); and the practice and judgment of art are not egalitarian and quantitative—except in the world of "pop art."

It may be replied, even by those who do not believe that whatever is is right: "So what? Misused words are only grit in the porridge, and such things have been assimilated for centuries. They don't spell doom." Well, grit in porridge is not agreeable to taste or digestion, and, consumed in quantity, may be fatal; since nowadays, as we have seen, there is no effective check on the spread of illiteracy, such particles—or should one say such pockets of fog?—multiply very rapidly and nourish carelessness, crudity and confusion not merely of expression but of thought. Easy tolerance of corruption recalls, in Thomas Love Peacock's *The Misfortunes of Elphin* (1829), a satirical flick at Tory opposition to electoral reform: refusing to repair a dike that was in a dangerous state of decay, the tipsy prince insisted: "But I say, the parts that are rotten give elasticity to those that are sound: they give elasticity, elasticity, elasticity. If it were all sound, it would break by its own obstinate stiffness."

We know that language is always changing and growing (and also, in a much smaller degree, shrinking), but acceptance of the perpetual process does not or should not mean blind surrender to the momentum or inertia of slovenly and tasteless ignorance and insensitivity. Ideally, changes should be inaugurated from above, by the masters of language (as they often have been), not from below. Language is not a tough plant that always grows toward the sun, regardless of weeds and trampling feet. From the Greeks (notably Plato) and Romans onward, many men of good will have been concerned about the use and abuse of language, the relations between the rhetoric of persuasion and private and public ethics, and all the attendant questions; and they did what they could to curb barbarism and foster taste, discipline and integrity. One great agent of discipline, though, has lost much or most of its traditional power. In our century and our country, and perhaps somewhat less conspicuously elsewhere, classical education, with the clear-eyed concreteness of mind it nourished (not that its products were all angels of light), has greatly declined, and, whatever the great virtues of modern writing, they are not an adequate substitute for some central and instinctive qualities of the ancients. One might call many witnesses on this point, Matthew Arnold, Santayana and others, but there is special aptness in some remarks of Evelyn Waugh, a contemporary and, whatever the general merits of his novels, a stylist of repute. In *A Little Learning: An Autobiography* (Boston, 1964), he thus sums up his schooling:

> My knowledge of English literature derived chiefly from my home. Most of my hours in the form room for ten years had been spent on Latin and Greek, History and Mathematics. Today I remember no Greek. I have never read Latin for pleasure and should now be hard put to it to compose a simple epitaph. But I do not regret my superficial classical studies. I believe that the conventional defence of them is valid; that only by them can a boy fully understand that a sentence is a logical construction and that words have basic inalienable meanings, departure from which is either conscious metaphor or inexcusable vulgarity. Those who have not been so taught—most Americans and most women— unless they are guided by some rare genius, betray their deprivation.

The old-fashioned test of an English sentence—will it translate?—still stands after we have lost the trick of translation. [P. 139]

A multitude of educated people (including teachers) do not seem to be deeply concerned about either language *per se* or its manifold implications. If we need illustrations of the obvious, we have evidence both rough and ready—or cloudy or slick—in the speech of many of our public men compared with that of many of their predecessors back through the seventeenth century; the urbane elegance of Adlai Stevenson was, in point of popular appeal, a heavy handicap in contrast to the amiable bumbling of General Eisenhower. It may be noted that the official proprietors of language, while they support uninhibited, uninstructed freedom in speech in opposition to what they regard as archaic rigidity, do not themselves—apart from occasional jargon—exploit the liberty they defend. That liberty, it appears, is both scientifically sound and in accord with the spirit of American democracy; it was not, however, the creed of the founding fathers and it belongs rather to the obsolete principle of *laissez faire*.

In the past, new words, new meanings, and new idioms had of necessity to undergo a period of probation; if they proved useful, they survived to enrich and refine the language. But the modern probationary period has greatly shrunk or vanished. Thanks especially to the mass media of the air, bad English can be established overnight, and not merely for the uneducated; it becomes current usage. (The same agencies, it may be added, help to inaugurate or propagate mispronunciation. We may wonder why nearly all Americans give a semi-French pronunciation to those age-old English names, Bernard and Maurice; or why the third edition of Webster, departing from the strictness of the second edition, accepts such common but quite unwarranted pronunciations as "skitsophrenia" and "par-li-a-ment.") And while on occasion opponents of "standard" English delve into the past for meanings not now approved by conservative orthodoxy, the same procedure must not be allowed to uphold the great mass of traditional words and idioms that remain or should remain standard if thought, feeling and communication are to carry their immense responsibility. Was it Churchill who said "When it is not necessary to change, it is necessary not to change"?

To the heterogeneous atoms of illiteracy that have been sampled might be added a different but related kind of bad English, although only a word can be said about its manifold varieties: that is, jargon. There is the simple jargon of pretentious padding, sometimes pseudo-technical: no one ever teaches in college but always "at the college level"; a crow is not black but basically or essentially black; nothing happens before anything else but always "prior to." No one feels pleasure or anxiety or fear; he feels a sense of pleasure, a sense of anxiety, a sense of fear. A politician doesn't say "Yes" but—if he is relatively forthright—"My answer is in the affirmative." Official and political rhetoric is not, of course, peculiar to our time or country. We remember that words are to be understood "in a Pickwickian sense"; we remember too Dickens' opinion of the parliamentary debates he reported. But it would appear that in modern times the mildew has grown much thicker. The recent death of Sir Alan Herbert recalls an example he once provided: if, he said, Nelson had lived during the Second World War, he would not have signaled to the fleet "England expects that every man will do his duty," but would have proclaimed: "England anticipates that as regards the current emergency, personnel will face up to the issues and exercise appropriately the functions allocated to their respective occupation groups." And we cannot forget that exquisite *jeu d'esprit* of an American journalist, the Gettysburg address rewritten in the style of General Eisenhower. On a less innocent level, political and official deception and downright lying may be accomplished directly (since the public is assumed to have a short memory) or through a smoke screen of evasive verbiage. Volumes could be filled with this kind of rhetoric, but the subject is too depressingly familiar to dwell upon.

A prime creator of "sophisticated" jargon has been advertising —who would not be allured by a baroque cocktail costume?—but that, like officialese, is too familiar to linger with. There are the kinds of jargon purveyed by the various tribes of scientists, social scientists and literary critics. While there are technical ideas and data that require a special language, it may be used to conceal a lack of ideas or to give thin ones impressive authority. I once had a visit from a bright and buoyant sophomore who, having received a C, wished to explain, first, that he was a Thomist in his thinking, and, secondly, that his writing, which I had termed clotted jargon, was "the English of the future"— a prophetic oracle that left me vanquished and dumb. Among parodies of psychological jargon a favorite of mine—because it exposes more than linguistic flatulence—is one that some readers may not have met, the opening of the Twenty-third Psalm, rendered by Alan Simpson, the president of Vassar College: "The Lord is my external, internal, integrated mechanism. I shall not be deprived of gratifications for my visceral generic hungers or my need dispositions. He motivates me to orient myself toward a nonsocial object effectiveness significance. He positions me in a nondecisional situation. He maximizes my adjustment." I read somewhere that Buster Keaton was asked by a sociologist in rotund polysyllabic language a question which, in brief, was whether his films tried to depict the plight of the little man in a bewildering world: said Keaton, after due reflection, "Well, we thought of a gag, and then we thought of another gag." For an early example of deflation we might go back to Chaucer's Franklin, who disclaimed any knowledge of "Colours of rethoryk": "For th'orisonte hath reft the sonne his lyght,—/This is as muche to seye as it was nyght!"

We have noticed only a few examples of the misuse of words and of the varieties of jargon that increasingly debase current English. We have not touched the abundance and vitality of clichés, which will not wear out "in the foreseeable future"; but this piece must "grind to a halt." For a final reminder of the illustrious past, we might recall Spenser's eulogy of "Dan Chaucer, well of English undefyled"; Mr. Auden was quoted at the outset; and there is T. S. Eliot's echo of Mallarmé, "To purify the dialect of the tribe" (*Little Gidding*). Language must be protected not only by poets but by the saving remnant of people who care—even though, as the flood rises, their role may be nearer King Canute's than Noah's.

Chapter 7

the closing of the universe
of discourse

Herbert Marcuse

> In the present state of history, all political writing can only confirm a police-universe, just as all intellectual writing can only produce para-literature which does not dare any longer to tell its name.
>
> *Roland Barthes*

The Happy Consciousness—the belief that the real is rational and that the system delivers the goods—reflects the new conformism which is a facet of technological rationality translated into social behavior. It is new because it is rational to an unprecedented degree. It sustains a society which has reduced—and in its most advanced areas eliminated—the more primitive irrationality of the preceding stages, which prolongs and improves life more regularly than before. The war of annihilation has not yet occurred; the Nazi extermination camps have been abolished. The Happy Consciousness repels the connection. Torture has been reintroduced as a normal affair, but in a colonial war which takes place at the margin of the civilized world. And there it is practiced with good conscience for war is war. And this war, too, is at the margin—it ravages only the "underdeveloped" countries. Otherwise, peace reigns.

The power over man which this society has acquired is daily absolved by its efficacy and productiveness. If it assimilates everything it touches, if it absorbs the opposition, if it plays with the contradiction, it demonstrates its cultural superiority. And in the same way the destruction of resources and the proliferation of waste demonstrate its opulence and the "high levels of well-being"; "the Community is too well off to care!" [1]

[1] John K. Galbraith, *American Capitalism* (Boston, Houghton Mifflin, 1956), p. 96.

THE LANGUAGE OF TOTAL ADMINISTRATION

This sort of well-being, the productive superstructure over the un-happy base of society, permeates the "media" which mediate between the masters and their dependents. Its publicity agents shape the universe of communication in which the one-dimensional behavior expresses itself. Its language testifies to identification and unification, to the systematic promotion of positive thinking and doing, to the concerted attack on transcendent, critical notions. In the prevailing modes of speech, the contrast appears between two-dimensional, dialectical modes of thought and technological behavior or social "habits of thought."

In the expression of these habits of thought, the tension between appearance and reality, fact and factor, substance and attribute tend to disappear. The elements of autonomy, discovery, demonstration, and critique recede before designation, assertion, and imitation. Magical, authoritarian and ritual elements permeate speech and language. Discourse is deprived of the mediations which are the stages of the process of cognition and cognitive evaluation. The concepts which comprehend the facts and thereby transcend the facts are losing their authentic linguistic representation. Without these mediations, language tends to express and promote the immediate identification of reason and fact, truth and established truth, essence and existence, the thing and its function.

These identifications, which appeared as a feature of operationalism, reappear as features of discourse in social behavior. Here functionalization of language helps to repel non-conformist elements from the structure and movement of speech. Vocabulary and syntax are equally affected. Society expresses its requirements directly in the linguistic material but not without opposition; the popular language strikes with spiteful and defiant humor at the official and semi-official discourse. Slang and colloquial speech have rarely been so creative. It is as if the common man (or his anonymous spokesman) would in his speech assert his humanity against the powers that be, as if the rejection and revolt, subdued in the political sphere, would burst out in the vocabulary that calls things by their names: "head-shrinker" and "egghead," "boob tube," "think tank," "beat it" and "dig it," and "gone, man, gone."

However, the defense laboratories and the executive offices, the governments and the machines, the time-keepers and managers, the efficiency experts and the political beauty parlors (which provide the leaders with the appropriate make-up) speak a different language and, for the time being, they seem to have the last word. It is the word that orders and organizes, that induces people to do, to buy, and to accept. It is transmitted in a style which is a veritable linguistic creation; a syntax in which the structure of the sentence is abridged and condensed in such a way that no tension, no "space" is left between the parts of the sentence. This linguistic form militates against a development of meaning. I shall presently try to illustrate this style.

The feature of operationalism—to make the concept synonymous with the corresponding set of operations—recurs in the linguistic tendency "to consider the names of things as being indicative at the same time of their manner of functioning, and the names of properties and processes as symbolical of the apparatus used to detect or produce them." [2] This is technological reasoning, which tends "to identify things and their functions." [3]

As a habit of thought outside the scientific and technical language, such reasoning shapes the expression of a specific social and political behaviorism. In this behavioral universe, words and concepts tend to coincide, or rather the concept tends to be absorbed by the word. The former has no other content than that designated by the word in the publicized and standardized usage, and the word is expected to have no other response than the publicized and standardized behavior (reaction). The word becomes *cliché* and, as cliché, governs the speech or the writing: the communication thus precludes genuine development of meaning.

To be sure, any language contains innumerable terms which do not require development of their meaning, such as the terms designating the objects and implements of daily life, visible nature, vital needs and wants. These terms are generally undertsood so that their mere appearance produces a response (linguistic or operational) adequate to the pragmatic context in which they are spoken.

The situation is very different with respect to terms which denote things or occurrences beyond this noncontroversial context. Here, the functionalization of language expresses an abridgment of meaning which has a political connotation. The names of things are not only "indicative of their manner of functioning," but their (actual) manner of functioning also defines and "closes" the meaning of the thing, excluding other manners of functioning. The noun governs

[2] Stanley Gerr, "Language and Science," in: *Philosophy of Science,* April 1942, p. 156.
[3] *Ibid.*

the sentence in an authoritarian and totalitarian fashion, and the sentence becomes a declaration to be accepted—it repels demonstration, qualification, negation of its codified and declared meaning.

At the nodal points of the universe of public discourse, self-validating, analytical propositions appear which function like magic-ritual formulas. Hammered and re-hammered into the recipient's mind, they produce the effect of enclosing it within the circle of the conditions prescribed by the formula.

I have already referred to the self-validating hypothesis as propositional form in the universe of political discourse. Such nouns as "freedom," "equality," "democracy," and "peace" imply, analytically, a specific set of attributes which occur invariably when the noun is spoken or written. In the West, the analytic predication is in such terms as free enterprise, initiative, elections, individual; in the East in terms of workers and peasants, building communism or socialism, abolition of hostile classes. On either side, transgression of the discourse beyond the closed analytical structure is incorrect or propaganda, although the means of enforcing the truth and the degree of punishment are very different. In this universe of public discourse, speech moves in synonyms and tautologies; actually, it never moves toward the qualitative difference. The analytic structure insulates the governing noun from those of its contents which would invalidate or at least disturb the accepted use of the noun in statements of policy and public opinion. The ritualized concept is made immune against contradiction.

Thus, the fact that the prevailing mode of freedom is servitude, and that the prevailing mode of equality is superimposed inequality is barred from expression by the closed definition of these concepts in terms of the powers which shape the respective universe of discourse. The result is the familiar Orwellian language ("peace is war" and "war is peace," etc.), which is by no means that of terroristic totalitarianism only. Nor is it any less Orwellian if the contradiction is not made explicit in the sentence but is enclosed in the noun. That a political party which works for the defense and growth of capitalism is called "Socialist," and a despotic government "democratic," and a rigged election "free" are familiar linguistic—and political—features which long predate Orwell.

Relatively new is the general acceptance of these lies by public and private opinion, the suppression of their monstrous content. The spread and the effectiveness of this language testify to the triumph of society over the contradictions which it contains; they are reproduced without exploding the social system. And it is the outspoken, blatant contradiction which is made into a device of speech and publicity. The syntax of abridgment proclaims the reconciliation of opposites by welding them together in a firm and familiar structure. I shall attempt to show that the "clean bomb" and the "harmless fall-out" are only the extreme creations of a normal style. Once considered the principal offense against logic, the contradiction now appears as a principle of the logic of manipulation—realistic caricature of dialectics. It is the logic of a society which can afford to dispense with logic and play with destruction, a society with technological mastery of mind and matter.

The universe of discourse in which the opposites are reconciled has a firm basis for such unification—its beneficial destructiveness. Total commercialization joins formerly antagonistic spheres of life, and this union expresses itself in the smooth linguistic conjunction of conflicting parts of speech. To a mind not yet sufficiently conditioned, much of the public speaking and printing appears utterly surrealistic. Captions such as "Labor is Seeking Missile Harmony," [4] and advertisements such as a "Luxury Fall-Out Shelter" [5] may still evoke the naïve reaction that "Labor," "Missile," and "Harmony" are irreconcilable contradictions, and that no logic and no language should be capable of correctly joining luxury and fall-out. However, the logic and the language become perfectly rational when we learn that a "nuclear-powered, ballistic-missile-firing submarine" "carries a price tag of $120,000,000" and that "carpeting, scrabble and TV" are provided in the $1,000 model of the shelter. The validation is not primarily in the fact that this language sells (it seems that the fall-out business was not so good) but rather that it promotes the immediate identification of the particular with the general interest, Business with National Power, prosperity with the annihilation potential. It is only a slip of the truth if a theater announces as a "Special Election Eve Perf., Strindberg's *Dance of Death*." [6] The announcement reveals the connection in a less ideological form than is normally admitted.

The unification of opposites which characterizes the commercial and political style is one of the many ways in which discourse and communication make themselves immune against the expression of protest and refusal. How can such protest and refusal find the right word when the organs of the established order admit and advertise that peace is really the brink of war, that the ultimate weapons carry

[4] *New York Times,* December 1, 1960.
[5] *Ibid.,* November 2, 1960.
[6] *Ibid.,* November 7, 1960.

their profitable price tags, and that the bomb shelter may spell coziness? In exhibiting its contradictions as the token of its truth, this universe of discourse closes itself against any other discourse which is not on its own terms. And, by its capacity to assimilate all other terms to its own, it offers the prospect of combining the greatest possible tolerance with the greatest possible unity. Nevertheless its language testifies to the repressive character of this unity. This language speaks in constructions which impose upon the recipient the slanted and abridged meaning, the blocked development of content, the acceptance of that which is offered in the form in which it is offered.

The analytic predication is such a repressive construction. The fact that a specific noun is almost always coupled with the same "explicatory" adjectives and attributes makes the sentence into a hypnotic formula which endlessly repeated, fixes the meaning in the recipient's mind. He does not think of essentially different (and possibly true) explications of the noun. Later we shall examine other constructions in which the authoritarian character of this language reveals itself. They have in common a telescoping and abridgement of syntax which cuts off development of meaning by creating fixed images which impose themselves with an overwhelming and petrified concreteness. It is the well-known technique of the advertisement industry, where it is methodically used for "establishing an image" which sticks to the mind and to the product, and helps to sell the men and the goods. Speech and writing are grouped around "impact lines" and "audience rousers" which convey the image. This image may be "freedom" of "peace," or the "nice guy" or the "communist" or "Miss Rheingold." The reader or listener is expected to associate (and does associate) with them a fixated structure of institutions, attitudes, aspirations, and he is expected to react in a fixated, specific manner.

Beyond the relatively harmless sphere of merchandising, the consequences are rather serious, for such language is at one and the same time "intimidation and glorification." [7] Propositions assume the form of suggestive commands—they are evocative rather than demonstrative. Predication becomes prescription; the whole communication has a hypnotic character. At the same time it is tinged with a false familiarity—the result of constant repetition, and of the skillfully managed popular directness of the communication. This relates itself to the recipient immediately—without distance of status, education, and office—and hits him or her in the informal atmosphere of the living room, kitchen, and bedroom.

[7] Roland Barthes, *Le Degré zéro de l'écriture* (Paris, Editions du Seuil, 1953), p. 33.

The same familiarity is established through personalized language, which plays a considerable role in advanced communication.[8] It is "your" congressman, "your" highway, "your" favorite drugstore, "your" newspaper; it is brought "to you," it invites "you," etc. In this manner, superimposed, standardized, and general things and functions are presented as "especially for you." It makes little difference whether or not the individuals thus addressed believe it. Its success indicates that it promotes the self-identification of the individuals with the functions which they and the others perform.

In the most advanced sectors of functional and manipulated communication, language imposes in truly striking constructions the authoritarian identification of person and function. *Time* magazine may serve as an extreme example of this trend. Its use of the inflectional genitive makes individuals appear to be mere appendices or properties of their place, their job, their employer, or enterprise. They are introduced as Virginia's Byrd, U. S. Steel's Blough, Egypt's Nasser. A hyphenated attributive construction creates a fixed syndrome:

> "Geogia's high-handed, low-browed governor . . . had the stage all set for one of his wild political rallies last week."

The governor,[9] his function, his physical features, and his political practices are fused together into one indivisible and immutable structure which, in its natural innocence and immediacy, overwhelms the reader's mind. The structure leaves no space for distinction, development, differentiation of meaning: it moves and lives only as a whole. Dominated by such personalized and hypnotic images, the article can then proceed to give even essential information. The narrative remains safely within the well-edited framework of a more or less human interest story as defined by the publisher's policy.

Use of the hyphenized abridgment is widespread. For example, "brush-browed" Teller, the "father of the H-bomb," "bull-shouldered missileman von Braun," "science-military dinner" [10] and the "nuclear-powered, ballistic-missile-firing" submarine. Such constructions are, perhaps not accidentally, particularly frequent in phrases joining technology, politics, and the military. Terms designating quite different spheres or qualities are forced together into a solid, overpowering whole.

The effect is again a magical and hypnotic one—the projection

---

[8] See Leo Lowenthal, *Literature, Popular Culture, and Society* (Prentice-Hall, 1961), p. 109 ff. and Richard Hoggart, *The Uses of Literacy* (Boston, Beacon Press, 1961), p. 161 ff.

[9] The statement refers, not to the present Governor, but to Mr. Talmadge.

[10] The last three items quoted in *The Nation*, Feb. 22, 1958.

of images which convey irresistible unity, harmony of contradictions. Thus the loved and feared Father, the spender of life, generates the H-bomb for the annihilation of life; "science-military" joins the efforts to reduce anxiety and suffering with the job of creating anxiety and suffering. Or, without the hyphen, the Freedom Academy of cold war specialists,[11] and the "clean bomb"—attributing to destruction moral and physical integrity. People who speak and accept such language seem to be immune to everything—and susceptible to everything. Hyphenation (explicit or not) does not always reconcile the irreconcilable; frequently, the combine is quite gentle—as in the case of the "bull-shouldered missileman"—or it conveys a threat, or an inspiring dynamic. But the effect is similar. The imposing structure unites the actors and actions of violence, power, protection, and propaganda in one lightning flash. We see the man or the thing in operation and only in operation—it cannot be otherwise.

Note on abridgment. NATO, SEATO, UN, AFL-CIO, AEC, but also USSR, DDR, etc. Most of these abbreviations are perfectly reasonable and justified by the length of the unabbreviated designata. However, one might venture to see in some of them a "cunning of Reason"—the abbreviation may help to repress undesired questions. NATO does not suggest what North Atlantic Treaty Organization says, namely, a treaty among the nations on the North-Atlantic—in which case one might ask questions about the membership of Greece and Turkey. USSR abbreviates Socialism and Soviet; DDR: democratic. UN dispenses with undue emphasis on "united"; SEATO with those Southeast-Asian countries which do not belong to it. AFL-CIO entombs the radical political differences which once separated the two organizations, and AEC is just one administrative agency among many others. The abbreviations denote that and only that which is institutionalized in such a way that the transcending connotation is cut off. The meaning is fixed, doctored, loaded. Once it has become an official vocable, constantly repeated in general usage, "sanctioned" by the intellectuals, it has lost all cognitive value and serves merely for recognition of an unquestionable fact.

This style is of an overwhelming *concreteness*. The "thing identified with its function" is more real than the thing distinguished from its function, and the linguistic expression of this identification

---

[11] A suggestion of *Life* magazine, quoted in *The Nation*, August 20, 1960. According to David Sarnoff, a bill to establish such an Academy is before Congress. See John K. Jessup, Adlai Stevenson, and others, *The National Purpose* (produced under the supervision and with the help of the editorial staff of *Life* magazine, New York, Holt, Rinehart and Winston, 1960), p. 58.

(in the functional noun, and in the many forms of syntactical abridgment) creates a basic vocabulary and syntax which stand in the way of differentation, separation, and distinction. This language, which constantly imposes *images*, militates against the development and expression of *concepts*. In its immediacy and directness, it impedes conceptual thinking; thus, it impedes thinking. For the concept does *not* identify the thing and its function. Such identification may well be the legitimate and perhaps even the only meaning of the operational and technological concept, but operational and technological definitions are specific usages of concepts for specific purposes. Moreover, they dissolve concepts in operations and exclude the conceptual intent which is opposed to such dissolution. Prior to its operational usage, the concept *denies* the identification of the thing with its function; it distinguishes that which the thing *is* from the contingent functions of the thing in the established reality.

The prevalent tendencies of speech, which repulse these distinctions, are expressive of the changes in the modes of thought discussed in the earlier chapters—the functionalized, abridged and unified language is the language of one-dimensional thought. In order to illustrate its novelty, I shall contrast it briefly with a classical philosophy of grammar which transcends the behavioral universe and relates linguistic to ontological categories.

According to this philosophy, the grammatical subject of a sentence is first a "substance" and remains such in the various states, functions, and qualities which the sentence predicates of the subject. It is actively or passively related to its predicates but remains different from them. If it is not a proper noun, the subject is more than a noun: it names the *concept* of a thing, a universal which the sentence defines as in a particular state or function. The grammatical subject thus carries a meaning in *excess* of that expressed in the sentence.

In the words of Wilhelm von Humboldt: the noun as grammatical subject denotes something that "can enter into certain relationships," [12] but is not identical with these relationships. Moreover, it remains what it is in and "against" these relationships; it is their "universal" and substantive core. The propositional synthesis links the action (or state) with the subject in such a manner that the subject is designated as the actor (or bearer) and thus is distinguished from the state or function in which it happens to be. In saying: "lightning strikes," one "thinks not merely of the striking lightning, but of the lightning itself which strikes," of a subject which "passed into ac-

---

[12] W. V. Humboldt, *Über die Verschiedenheit des menschlichen Sprachbaues*, reprint Berlin 1936, p. 254.

tion." And if a sentence gives a definition of its subject, it does not dissolve the subject in its states and functions, but defines it as being in this state, or exercising this function. Neither disappearing in its predicates nor existing as an entity before and outside its predicates, the subject constitutes itself in its predicates—the result of a process of mediation which is expressed in the sentence.[13]

I have alluded to the philosophy of grammar in order to illuminate the extent to which the linguistic abridgments indicate an abridgment of thought which they in turn fortify and promote. Insistence on the philosophical elements in grammar, on the link between the grammatical, logical, and ontological "subject," points up the contents which are suppressed in the functional language, barred from expression and communication. Abridgment of the concept in fixed images; arrested development in self-validating, hypnotic formulas; immunity against contradiction; identification of the thing (and of the person) with its function—these tendencies reveal the one-dimensional mind in the language it speaks.

If the linguistic behavior blocks conceptual development, if it militates against abstraction and mediation, if it surrenders to the immediate facts, it repels recognition of the factors behind the facts, and thus repels recognition of the facts, and of their historical content. In and for the society, this organization of functional discourse is of vital importance; it serves as a vehicle of coordination and subordination. The unified, functional language is an irreconcilably anti-critical and anti-dialectical language. In it, operational and behavioral rationality absorbs the transcendent, negative, oppositional elements of Reason.

I shall discuss these elements in terms of the tension between the "is" and the "ought," between essence and appearance, potentiality and actuality—ingression of the negative in the positive determinations of logic. This sustained tension permeates the two-dimensional universe of discourse which is the universe of critical, abstract thought. The two dimensions are antagonistic to each other; the reality partakes of both of them, and the dialectical concepts develop the real contradictions. In its own development, dialectical thought came to comprehend the historical character of the contradictions and the process of their mediation as historical process. Thus the "other" dimension of thought appeared to be *historical* dimension—the potentiality as historical possibility, its realization as historical event.

[13] See for this philosophy of grammar in dialectical logic Hegel's concept of the "substance as subject" and of the "speculative sentence" in the Preface to the *Phaenomenology of the Spirit.*

The suppression of this dimension in the societal universe of operational rationality is a *suppression of history,* and this is not an academic but a political affair. It is suppression of the society's own past—and of its future, inasmuch as this future invokes the qualitative change, the negation of the present. A universe of discourse in which the categories of freedom have become interchangeable and even identical with their opposites is not only practicing Orwellian or Aesopian language but is repulsing and forgetting the historical reality—the horror of fascism; the idea of socialism; the preconditions of democracy; the content of freedom. If a bureaucratic dictatorship rules and defines communist society, if fascist regimes are functioning as partners of the Free World, if the welfare program of enlightened capitalism is successfully defeated by labeling it "socialism," if the foundations of democracy are harmoniously abrogated in democracy, then the old historical concepts are invalidated by up-to-date operational redefinitions. The redefinitions are falsifications which, imposed by the powers that be and the powers of fact, serve to transform falsehood into truth.

The functional language is a radically anti-historical language: operational rationality has little room and little use for historical reason.[14] Is this fight against history part of the fight against a dimension of the mind in which centrifugal faculties and forces might develop—faculties and forces that might hinder the total coordination of the individual with the society? Remembrance of the past may give rise to dangerous insights, and the established society seems to be apprehensive of the subversive contents of memory. Remembrance is a mode of dissociation from the given facts, a mode of "mediation" which breaks, for short moments, the omnipresent power of the given facts. Memory recalls the terror and the hope that passed. Both come to life again, but whereas in reality, the former recurs in ever new forms, the latter remains hope. And in the personal events which reappear in the individual memory, the fears and aspirations of mankind assert themselves—the universal in the particular. It is history which memory preserves. It succumbs to the totalitarian power of the behavioral universe:

> Das "Schreckbild einer Menschheit ohne Erinnerung . . . ist kein
> blosses Verfallsprodukt . . . sondern es ist mit der Fortschrittlichkeit

[14] This does not mean that history, private or general, disappears from the universe of discourse. The past is evoked often enough: be it as the Founding Fathers, or Marx-Engels-Lenin, or as the humble origins of a presidential candidate. However these too, are ritualized invocations which do not allow development of the content recalled; frequently, the mere invocation serves to block such development, which would show its historical impropriety.

des bügerlichen Prinzips notwendig verknüpft." "Oekonomen und
Soziologen wie Werner Sombart und Max Weber haben das Prinzip des
Traditionalismus den feudalen Gesellschaftsformen zugeordnet und das
der Rationalität den bürgerlichen. Das sagt aber nicht weniger, als dass
Erinnerung, Zeit, Gedächtnis von der fortschreitenden bürgerlichen
Gesellschaft selber als eine Art irrationaler Rest liquidiert wird . . ." [15]

If the progressing rationality of advanced industrial society tends
to liquidate, as an "irrational rest," the disturbing elements of Time
and Memory, it also tends to liquidate the disturbing rationality con-
tained in this irrational rest. Recognition and relation to the past
as present counteracts the functionalization of thought by and in the
established reality. It militates against the closing of the universe of discourse and behavior; it renders possible the development of concepts
which de-stabilize and transcend the closed universe by comprehending
it as historical universe. Confronted with the given society as object
of its reflection, critical thought becomes historical consciousness; as
such, it is essentially judgment. Far from necessitating an indifferent
relativism, it searches in the real history of man for the criteria of truth
and falsehood, progress and regression. The mediation of the past
with the present discovers the factors which made the facts, which
determined the way of life, which established the masters and the servants; it projects the limits and the alternatives. When this critical
consciousness speaks, it speaks "le langage de la connaissance" (Roland
Barthes) which breaks open a closed universe of discourse and its
petrified structure. The key terms of this language are not hypnotic
nouns which evoke endlessly the same frozen predicates. They rather
allow of an open development; they even unfold their content in contradictory predicates.

The Communist Manifesto provides a classical example. Here
the two key terms, Bourgeoisie and Proletariat, each "govern" contrary predicates. The "bourgeoisie" is the subject of technical progress,
liberation, conquest of nature, creation of social wealth, *and* of the
perversion and destruction of these achievements. Similarly, the "proletariat" carries the attributes of total oppression *and* of the total de-
feat of oppression.

Such dialectical relation of opposites in and by the proposition

[15] "The spectre of man without memory . . . is more than an aspect of decline—it is necessarily linked with the principle of progress in bourgeois society."
"Economists and sociologists such as Werner Sombart and Max Weber correlated the
principle of tradition to feudal, and that of rationality to bourgeois, forms of society.
This means no less than that the advancing bourgeois society liquidates Memory,
Time, Recollection as irrational leftovers of the past . . ." Th. W. Adorno, "Wes
bedeutet Anfarbeitung der Vergangenheit?," in Bericht über die Erzieherkonferenz
am 6 und 7. November in Wiesbaden; Frankfurt 1960, p. 14.

is rendered possible by the recognition of the subject as an historical agent whose identity constitutes itself in *and against* its historical practice, in *and against* its social reality. The discourse develops and states the conflict between the thing and its function, and this conflict finds linguistic expression in sentences which join contradictory predicates in a logical unit—conceptual counterpart of the objective reality. In contrast to all Orwellian language, the contradiction is demonstrated, made explicit, explained, and denounced.

I have illustrated the contrast between the two languages by referring to the style of Marxian theory, but the critical, cognitive qualities are not the exclusive characteristics of the Marxian style. They can also be found (though in different modes) in the style of the great conservative and liberal critique of the unfolding bourgeois society. For example, the language of Burke and Tocqueville on the one side, of John Stuart Mill on the other is a highly demonstrative, conceptual, "open" language, which has not yet succumbed to the hypnotic-ritual formulas of present-day neo-conservatism and neo-liberalism.

However, the authoritarian ritualization of discourse is more striking where it affects the dialectical language itself. The requirements of competitive industrialization, and the total subjection of man to the productive apparatus appears in the authoritarian transformation of the Marxist into the Stalinist and post-Stalinist language. These requirements, as interpreted by the leadership which controls the apparatus, define what is right and wrong, true and false. They leave no time and no space for a discussion which would project disruptive alternatives. This language no longer lends itself to "discourse" at all. It pronounces and, by virtue of the power of the apparatus, establishes facts—it is self-validating enunciation. Here,[16] it must suffice to quote and paraphrase the passage in which Roland Barthes describes its magic-authoritarian features: "il n'y a plus aucun sursis entre la dénomination et le jugement, et la clôture du langage est parfaite . . ." [17]

The closed language does not demonstrate and explain—it communicates decision, dictum, command. Where it defines, the definition becomes "separation of good from evil"; it establishes unquestionable rights and wrongs, and one value as justification of another value. It moves in tautologies, but the tautologies are terribly effective "sentences." They pass judgment in a "prejudged form"; they pronounce condemnation. For example, the "objective content," that is, the defi-

---

[16] See my *Soviet Marxism*.

[17] "there is no longer any delay between the naming and the judgment, and the closing of the language is complete."

nition of such terms as "deviationist," "revisionist," is that of the penal code, and this sort of validation promotes a consciousness for which the language of the powers that be is the language of truth.[18]

Unfortunately, this is not all. The productive growth of the established communist society also condemns the libertarian communist opposition; the language which tries to recall and preserve the original truth succumbs to its ritualization. The orientation of discourse (and action) on terms such as "the proletariat," "workers' councils," the "dictatorship of the Stalinist apparatus," becomes orientation on ritual formulas where the "proletariat" no longer or not yet exists, where direct control "from below" would interfere with the progress of mass production, and where the fight against the bureaucracy would weaken the efficacy of the only real force that can be mobilized against capitalism on an international scale. Here the past is rigidly retained but not mediated with the present. One opposes the concepts which comprehended a historical situation without developing them into the present situation—one blocks their dialectic.

The ritual-authoritarian language spreads over the contemporary world, through democratic and non-democratic, capitalist and non-capitalist countries.[19] According to Roland Barthes, it is the language "propre à tous les régimes d'autorité," and is there today, in the orbit of advanced industrial civilization, a society which is not under an authoritarian regime? As the substance of the various regimes no longer appears in alternative modes of life, it comes to rest in alternative techniques of manipulation and control. Language not only reflects these controls but becomes itself an instrument of control even where it does not transmit orders but information; where it demands, not obedience but choice, not submission but freedom.

This language controls by reducing the linguistic forms and symbols of reflection, abstraction, development, contradiction; by substituting images for concepts. It denies or absorbs the transcendent vocabulary; it does not search for but establishes and imposes truth and falsehood. But this kind of discourse is not terroristic. It seems unwarranted to assume that the recipients believe, or are made to believe, what they are being told. The new touch of the magic-ritual language rather is that people don't believe it, or don't care, and yet

[18] Roland Barthes, *loc. cit.*, pp. 37–40.

[19] For West Germany see the intensive studies undertaken by the Institut für Sozialforschung, Frankfurt am Main, in 1950–1951: *Gruppen Experiment*, ed. F. Pollock (Frankfurt, Europaeische Verlagsanstalt, 1955) esp. p. 545 f. Also Karl Korn, *Sprache in der verwalteten Welt* (Frankfurt, Heinrich Scheffler, 1958), for both parts of Germany.

act accordingly. One does not "believe" the statement of an operational concept but it justifies itself in action—in getting the job done, in selling and buying, in refusal to listen to others, etc.

If the language of politics tends to become that of advertising, thereby bridging the gap between two formerly very different realms of society, then this tendency seems to express the degree to which domination and administration have ceased to be a separate and independent function in the technological society. This does not mean that the power of the professional politicians has decreased. The contrary is the case. The more global the challenge they build up in order to meet it, the more normal the vicinity of total destruction, the greater their freedom from effective popular sovereignty. But their domination has been incorporated into the daily performances and relaxation of the citizens, and the "symbols" of politics are also those of business, commerce, and fun.

The vicissitudes of the language have their parallel in the vicissitudes of political behavior. In the sale of equipment for relaxing entertainment in bomb shelters, in the television show of competing candidates for national leadership, the juncture between politics, business, and fun is complete. But the juncture is fraudulent and fatally premature—business and fun are still the politics of domination. This is not the satire-play after the tragedy; it is not *finis tragoediae*—the tragedy may just begin. And again, it will not be the hero but the people who will be the ritual victims.

Chapter 8

format and "communications"

Paul Goodman

1. FORMAT AND EMPTY SPEECH

By "format" I mean imposing on the literary process a style that is extrinsic to it. The dictionary tells the history very well:

> Format. —*n*. 1. the shape and size of a book as determined by the number of times the original sheet has been folded to form the leaves. 2. the general physical appearance of a book, magazine, or newspaper, such as the type face, binding, quality of paper, margins, etc. 3. the organization, plan, style, or type of something: *They tailored their script to a half-hour format. The format of the show allowed for topical and controversial gags.* 4. *Computer Technol.* the organization or disposition of symbols on a magnetic tape, punch card, or the like, in accordance with the input requirements of a computer, card-sort machine, etc. —*v.t.* 5. *Computer Technol.* to adapt (the organization or disposition of coded information) on a magnetic tape, punch card, or the like, to conform to the input requirements of a computer, card-sort machine, etc.

Format has no literary power, and finally it destroys literary power. It is especially disastrous to the common standard style, because it co-opts it and takes the heart out of it.

Thus, an editor chops a sentence here and there, and also my last paragraph, because 3,000 words is the right length for the format of his magazine. An assistant editor rewrites me just to be busy and earn his keep. A daily column must appear though the columnist has

"Format and 'Communications.'" From Paul Goodman, *Speaking and Language: Defense of Poetry* (New York: Random House, 1971), pp. 200–215. Copyright © 1971 by Paul Goodman. Reprinted by permission of Random House, Inc.

nothing to say that day. An editor of *Harper's* asks me to simplify an argument because, he says, the readers of the magazine cannot digest more than two thoughts to one article. At another magazine they re-write in Time-style. A young fellow writes his thesis in the style of professional competence of his department. Obviously, the effect of format is worse if the writer must adapt himself and write, rather than just having his writing mashed. Since writing is inherently spontane-ous and original, a writer cannot produce what is not his own without a broken spirit.

American television is especially productive of format. The net-works are a big investment of capital, so broadcasting time is cut up for sale to the fraction of a minute, and programs are tailored to the strips. A mass medium aims at a big audience, so the programs must be sensational enough to attract many and bland enough not to offend any. In the peculiar system of semi-monopolies, where a few baronial firms compete in such a way as to keep one another in business, if one network hits on a new show or newscast, the others at once program a close imitation. Legally the channels are public property, so the licensed stations must be politically impartial and present all sides of controversial issues; the most convenient way of handling this is to pre-sent no controversial issue. But there is another rule that a certain fraction of time must be devoted to public service, including political controversy; and a way of economically handling this is to have a panel of wildly divergent points of view debating an issue for the re-quired twenty-six minutes. This sometimes produces heat, never light, usually nothing. It is a format. What is glaring in the whole enter-prise is the almost entire lack of will to *say* anything, rather than just provide a frame for the ads.[1]

Format is not like censorship that tries to obliterate speech, and so sometimes empowers it by making it important. And it is not like propaganda that simply tells lies. Rather, authority imposes format on speech because it needs speech, but not autonomous speech. Format is speech colonized, broken-spirited. It is a use of speech as social-cement, but it is not like the small talk of acquaintances on the street in their spontaneous style; it is a collective style for a mass. So in appearance it is often indistinguishable from the current literary standard. But in

---

[1] In my fallible memory, the ads themselves used to have a more authentic style—more cinematic, more musical, even more poetical—because they had a real rhetorical purpose, to sell goods. But my recent observation is that they too have become lifeless. Is this because of the imposition of new extrinsic regulations, e.g. not to lie, not to sell carcinogens or dangerous toys, not to increase air pollution, etc.? It is hard to be a frank huckster anymore.

actual use it is evident from the first sentence that it does not tell anything.

Of course, empty style is nothing new. Diplomats, administrators of all kinds, and other public relators, who have to make remarks about what is none of our business, have always used a style to drain meaning from what they say. It can be a fine art—cf. Proust on the virtuosity of Norpois. But modern society has unique resources of technology and social organization to separate speech from living speakers. I do not think that any previous era has ever worked up a universal pedagogy and a general Theory of Communications to side-track human speech as such. In Newspeak, George Orwell was shooting at not quite the right target. He was thinking of *control* of speech by the lies and propaganda of crude totalitarian regimes; but I doubt that this is humanly feasible. (In the end the State is bound together by simple fright, not brainwashing.) The government of a complicated modern society cannot lie *much*. But by format, even without trying, it can kill feeling, memory, learning, observation, imagination, logic, grammar, or any other faculty of free writing.

2

The schools try hard to teach the empty style. There is frantic anxiety about the schools' failing to teach children to read and write; there have been riots on the street about it; the President of the United States has called the matter our top priority. But so far as I know, none of those who are frantic—parents rich and poor, nor the President—have pointed out that reading and writing spring from speaking, our human way of being in the world; that they are not tools but arts, and their content is imagination and truth. Occasionally a sensitive teacher pipes up that children might learn reading and writing if these were interesting and sprang from what the children wanted to know and had to say, if they were relevant to their personal lives and had some practical function. But mostly the remedies that are proposed are mechanical or administrative; there are debates between sounding out and word recognition and quarrels about who controls the schools.

The reason for anxiety is simply that if children do not learn the tools of reading and writing, they cannot advance through school, and if they don't get school diplomas, they won't get well-paying jobs in a mandarin society. Literacy is incidental, a kind of catalyst that drops out of the equation. To pass the tests really requires just the

same verbal skills—nothing much else has been learned—and there is
no correlation between having the diplomas and competence in any
job or profession. School style exists for the schools. So some of us
have suggested that if it and they did not exist, that too would be
very well. (Rather, change the rules for licensing and hiring.)

In most urban and suburban communities, most children will
pick up the printed code anyway, school or no school. (In ghetto and
depressed rural communities, they might not.) It is likely that school-
teaching destroys more genuine literacy than it produces. But it is
hard to know if most people think that reading and writing have any
value anyway, either in themselves or for their use, except that they
are indispensable in how we go about things. Contrast the common
respect for mathematics, which are taken to be *about* something and
are powerful, productive, magical; yet there is no panic if people are
mathematically illiterate.

Thus, during the long years of compulsory schooling, reading
and writing are a kind of format, an imposed style with no intrinsic
relation to good speech. And this must be characteristic of any mandarin society, even when, as in medieval China, the style of literacy happens to be the standard literary classics. With us, as school reading and
writing cease to have literary meaning, university study of Literature
ceases to be about human speech, speech in its great examples. (It is a
nice question, what university English studies *are* about.) And as
fewer people read authentically, on-going literature may well become
one of the minor arts, for connoisseurs, like rose gardening or weaving.

Naturally, when the imposing authority takes itself seriously as
right and good, as in the Soviet Union, mandarin literacy is affirmed
as excellent, the vehicle of all social and scientific progress, as well as
the way to get ahead. Consider the following of the Russian peda-
gogue L. S. Vygotsky, which seems to say that it is necessary to *destroy*
natural style:

> In learning to write, the child must disengage himself from the sensory
> aspect of speech and replace words by images of words. It is the abstract
> quality of language that is the main stumbling block to learning to
> write, not the underdevelopment of small muscles. . . . Our studies
> show that a child has little motivation to learn writing when we begin
> to teach it. Written language demands conscious work. . . . The con-
> crete totality of traits [must be] destroyed through abstraction; then the
> possibility of unifying traits on a different basis opens up. Only the
> mastery of abstraction enables the child to progress to the formation of
> genuine concepts.

This odd view of writing and teaching writing is the precise opposite
of a literary approach, e.g. Sylvia Ashton-Warner's, which tries to get

writing from the child's spontaneous native speech, with all its sensuality and animal need. (We shall see later that by "genuine concepts" Vygotsky means the social ideology.)[2]

The use of words is already detachment from, control of, the stream of experience; to go the further step of Vygotsky is to control the speaker. It is a socially-induced aphasia.

In any case, the literature that is the fruit of this method of teaching writing is also taken very seriously, as the mandarin literacy is. It is carefully regulated in style, and it is reproduced in millions of copies. In Russia, writing that is more literary in a traditional sense does *not* become a minor art for connoisseurs, but is circulated in manuscript for a band of criminal conspirators.

3. THE RESISTANCE OF COLLOQUIAL SPEECH

The forces of format, "to conform to the input requirements" of a social or technical system, can quickly debase public language and the standard literary style. Strong writers are less affected; society does not know how to produce them and it does not even know how to inhibit them, except by violence.

But colloquial speech is quite impervious to corruption by format. It has an irrepressible vitality to defy, ridicule, or appropriate. It gobbles up format like everything else. There are too many immediate occasions, face-to-face meetings, eye-witnessings, common sense problems, for common speech to be regimented. People who can talk can be oppressed but not brainwashed. Modern cities are depressing and unhealthy, but the people are not mechanical.

Once out of bounds, children do not talk like school. In America, adults talk like school less than they used, because (I like to think) the school style has so little literary value that it's not worth adopting. Children imitate the TV, but soon do it sarcastically. Adults imitate the ads less than they used because there has been overexposure. The young are in revolt against the ads, so the ads lamely have to imitate the young. In totalitarian countries, even after a generation of benevolent instruction by all the schools, mass media, labor unions, etc.,

---

[2] It is astonishing that Vygotsky can believe what he says. In another passage he shrewdly and accurately points out how the school set-up predetermines the child's responses: "Piaget's findings are valid only for his special kindergarten play milieu [encouraging] extensive soliloquizing. Stern points out that in a German kindergarten, where there is more group activity, the coefficient of egocentrism was somewhat lower. . . . The difference with Soviet children must be even greater." Indeed, in *all* cases a child must cope with the conditions that they impose on him, and re-adjust in order to survive. To do *this* is the child's nature.

young Czechs and Poles, who have never known any other dispensation, have not learned what is good for them; apparently, they get their ideas by conversation with one another. American voters almost never repeat the sentences of politicians; rather, they tell you their own lay political theories and that they can't stand the personalities of certain candidates.

By and large, adolescents are the most susceptible to empty format. They often seem to take TV images for reality. In serious moments they often sound like a textbook in social psychology: A girl has a "meaningful relationship with her boy friend," people are "consumed by negative feelings toward someone in the group"—I am quoting from *WIN,* the best of the youth movement magazines. And it is amazing how the language of underground newspapers, identical by dozens, is actually spoken by teen-agers. But this language is less format than it seems. It is filling the vacuum of adolescent speechlessness. The stereotypes serve as glue for ganging together, and the ganging is real though the language is spurious. A rock festival is usually a commercial hoax, but the pilgrimage to it is not.

More poignant is the speech of a highly articulate, but unread, militant *chicano* housewife, who declaims social-worker Newspeak during a demonstration because she has no other public words. But her passion gives it life, if not sense.

The deep pathos of colloquial speech—with its indestructible good sense, eye-witnessing, communal vitality, and crotchetiness (including much private error and deeprooted tribal prejudice)—is that in highly organized societies its field of operation is strictly limited. We can speak good colloquial where we have freedom to initiate and decide. When our actions are predetermined by institutional and political frameworks that are imposed on us, we necessarily become anxious, inconfident of ourselves, and we fall into institutional and ideological format and its mesmerized thoughts. Thus in our societies there is continually spoken a dual language: Intimately, people talk sense—about politics, the commodities, the schools, the police, etc.—yet they also talk format, and act on it. In totalitarian societies, where a strong effort is made to reform colloquial speech to official format, the effort cannot succeed, but people do begin to whisper and fall silent; finally, only a few brave writers, who have a very special obligation to honorable speech, continue to talk like human beings.[3]

---

[3] Fortunately, there is hard evidence for my conjecture that modern people aren't "dehumanized." The Princeton Theological Seminary ran an ingenious experiment that showed that students stopped to help a (planted) man in need or passed him by not because of their gentleness or hardness of heart, but because they were told they had time or were late for an examination. Frederic Darley and

In America, our colloquial is certainly not much improved by respectable literary models. It is a loss, because people would express themselves more clearly and forcefully if they could express themselves a little more literarily yet without sounding like a book, and they could thereby also extend the boundaries of their human expression into more public domains—at least somewhat (there would be conflict). A few of us writers do the best we can. Some of the young pick up our language—and turn in into *their* format!

There *is* a kind of style to our speech. It is the style of urban confusion: a Yiddish that chews up and can assimilate the ads, the sociological jargon, the political double-talk, the canned entertainment.

To achieve the controlled and accurate transmission of messages, it is necessary finally to dispense with human speakers altogether, and let us now turn our attention to this.

4. "COMMUNICATIONS"

The primary idea of the art of communications is to open channels or provide technical means by which speakers can talk to one another, like couriers or telegraph or telephone. As the general Theory of Communications has developed, however—it is a new branch of philosophy —the idea has come to be to make the signals precise and perfectly transmissible by explaining away the speakers. I will briefly trace the steps of this curious outcome, quoting from some of the chief authors.

Most simply, and innocently, whenever we use any medium or technical means to convey our meaning, there must be some adjustment of the form of the message to be handled by the medium or the technology. An engineer of the telephone company who wants to improve reception of the signals will urge speakers to say the phonemes sharply, and he might suggest new pronunciations for very frequent words: "faiəv" for "five," "naiən" for "nine." The speakers must not speak too quick, too slow, too loud, too soft. In the fine arts, of course, the adaptation to the medium is what the whole art is about: The "object of imitation" must assume an entirely new form and live and

---

Gregory Bateson suggest that the Good Samaritan of the parable was probably in a "low hurry" condition, while the priest and Levite were doubtlessly rushing: "One can imagine the priest and Levite, prominent public figures, hurrying along with little black books full of meetings and appointments, glancing furtively at their sun dials as they go. In contrast, the Samaritan, a man of much lower public status, would likely have fewer and less important people counting on him to be at a set place at a set time."

breathe in the medium. From this beginning, the theorists at once take a giant step.

> Words [says Julian Huxley] are tools for dealing more efficiently with the business of existence; so that language is properly speaking a branch of technology.

Here the words are not adapted to the technology, they are themselves the technology. In this formulation, speaking is not to be considered as itself one of the free human actions—it is a means to expedite other actions. (One wonders what they are.) The study of language is suddenly no longer one of the humanities.

Regarding language as a technology, we can begin to refine what it must be.

> The communications engineer [says Roman Jakobson . . .] most properly approaches the essence of the speech event when he assumes that the optimal speaker and listener have at their disposal more or less the same "filing cabinet of prefabricated representations"; the addressor selects one of these preconceived possibilities and the addressee is supposed to make an identical choice from the same assembly of possibilities already foreseen and provided for.

Needless to say, this is a very different doctrine from what I have been calling either the literary process or colloquial speech, where the speaker, drawing on many powers and expressing his needs, modifies the language to fit the unique situation. But if speakers cannot creatively adjust to the conversation they are having, Jakobson's requirement is certainly a technological necessity for accurate transmission. Otherwise there will be guessing and sometimes not grasping what is meant at all, as if it were a foreign language.

It is in this sense that we must understand Jakobson's remark that

> The efficiency of a speech event demands the use of a common code by the participants.

The common code is not what the speakers have as a convenience, as they might have other common possessions; it is what they have as a law, that they must not tamper with. We have commented on many passages of Saussure and the cultural anthropologists, how this code is constant, supra-individualistic, and generalized. In the extreme view of Whorf, it predetermines what the speakers must think.

But next, according to Count Korzybski, we can make a more precise specification for the prefabricated representations that fill the filing cabinets and are the common code. They are, says the Count, the names of "facts" organized into classes and classes of classes, in levels of abstraction. Using abstractions

> integrates the cortico-thalamic functions [by] inducing an automatic delay of reactions which automatically stimulates the cortical region and regulates and protects the usually over-stimulated thalamic region.

On this theory, the use of right speech would preclude any forceful action or final satisfaction of life, for these always have concrete objects and becomes spontaneous. He seems to be describing what I call "acting in a chronic low-grade emergency"—cf. *Gestalt Therapy* (II, iii, 9, and II, xi, 4). But he tells us,

> The socio-cultural developments of civilization depend on the capacity to produce higher and higher abstractions.

Freud called this *Civilization and Its Discontents*.

For the pedagogy to teach this common code of higher abstractions, we return to L. S. Vygotsky:

> We define "consciousness" to denote awareness of the activity of the mind, the consciousness of being conscious. . . . A concept can become subject to consciousness and deliberate control only when it is part of a system. If consciousness means generalizing, generalization in turn means the formation of a superordinate concept that includes the concept as a case. A superordinate concept implies the existence of a series of subordinates and a hierarchy. Thus the concept is placed within a system of relationships of generality. . . . In the scientific concepts that the child acquires in school, the relationship to an object is mediated from the start by some other concept. It is our contention that the rudiments of systematization first enter the child's mind by way of his contact with scientific concepts of the [teacher] and are then transferred to everyday concepts, changing their psychological structure from the top down. This is why certain thoughts cannot be communicated to children, even if they are familiar with the necessary words.[4]

Here at last is a prescription for transforming common speech itself into format. Just browbeat the child with verbal explanations that he cannot understand. Vygotsky spells it out in a remarkable example:

> A child cannot use "because" in real life situations, but he can correctly finish sentences on social science subjects, e.g. "Planned economy is possible in the Soviet Union because there is no private property—

---

[4] It is interesting, but not surprising, that Kropotkin, who was an anarchist, makes exactly the contrary point: You can teach anything to a child or an unlearned peasant *if you yourself* understand it concretely and therefore can follow *his* understanding and offer it by the right handle.

all lands, factories, and plants belong to the workers and peasants."
Why is he capable of performing the operation in this case? Because the
teacher, working with the pupil, has explained, supplied information,
questioned, corrected, and made the pupil explain. Later, in finishing
the sentence about his bicycle, he makes use of the fruits of that collabo-
ration, this time independently. . . . With the progressive isolation of
speech for oneself, vocalization becomes unnecessary, and because of its
growing structural peculiarities also impossible. In reality, however,
behind the symptoms of dissolution [of common speech] lies a progressive development, the birth of a new speech form.

This new speech is mandarin or format. Orwell was not thinking of
anything nearly so sophisticated, in describing Newspeak. The trick of
breaking the free spirit that is inherent in speaking is "to make the
pupil explain." The way of breaking the spirit of a writer is to pay
him to write what makes no sense to him in a style that is not his own.

I have quoted at length from the Russian savant partly for his
dogged manner but especially because he adequately brings us to another great leap in the Theory of Communications—the elimination
of speakers because they are supernumeraries. Since we have nullified
the free action of speakers, their realm of choice, their individuality,
their thalamic emotions, and their concrete experience, and since their
thoughts are internalizations of top-down instruction in a system of
generalizations, it is possible to lop them off with Ockham's razor and
to say that communication is the transaction of the system of general
signs. This is what Sir Julian Huxley does:

> Language provides a new environment for life to inhabit. I shall call it
> the Noösphere, after Teilhard de Chardin. As fish swim in the sea and
> birds fly in the air, so we think and feel our way through this collective
> mental world.

The Noösphere, in Teilhard, is the network of signals which has
evolved to brood over the world like the program of a universal computer—the Abbé identifies it with Jesus.

(It is remarkable how, pushed to the extreme, the technological
approach to language converges so exactly, in content and rhetoric,
with the anti-technological humanism of the phenomenologists, pushed
to the extreme; cf. Merleau-Ponty's "Speech is like an *être,* like a universe. It is never limited except by further language." In the end, it
makes little difference if the "collective mental world" is man's new
environment, or a project of freedom, or, as with Vygotsky, the in-
ternalized ideology of the State. But none of these describes what it is
like to speak a language.)

It remains only for the physical world, too, to become Communications, and this step is taken by Norbert Wiener, with the synoptic

elegance of a mathematician. The form or pattern of matter, the ordering of entropy (= disorder), is information; to cause such patterns is communication:

> When I control the actions of another person, I communicate a message to him, although the message is in the imperative mood. . . . The commands through which we exercise control over our environment are a kind of information which we impart to it. . . . Information is a name for the content of what is exchanged with the outer world as we adjust to it and make our adjustment felt upon it.

Putting it this way, moreover, we could say that a bat communicates with the ball it hits; there is no reason to take the point of view that "we," human beings, are the communicators; there is nothing essential to the metaphor "inner" and "outer." Indeed, a human being may well be the *message:*

> The organism is seen as a message. Organism is opposed to chaos, to disintegration, to death, as message is to noise. To describe an organism we answer certain questions about it which reveal its pattern. It is the pattern maintained by homeostasis which is the touchstone of our personal identity—and this may be transmitted as a message, e.g. by wire. [To be sure,] any scanning of the human organism must be a probe going through all its parts, and will accordingly tend to destroy the tissue on its way. To hold an organism stable while part of it is being slowly destroyed, with the intention of creating it out of other material elsewhere . . . in most cases would destroy life. In other words, the fact that we cannot telegraph the pattern of a man seems to be due to technical difficulties—the idea itself is highly plausible.

Wiener does not envisage the man as a respondent or speaker who might interpret what is going on or object to it, for instance by saying "Ouch!" If he would say "Ouch!" however, would not this continually interject new information and put the scanner always one step behind?

Thus, I have brought together half a dozen passages by important authors to show the kind of thing that sets my teeth on edge in modern theory of language. But I am sorry to conclude with a passage from Norbert Wiener, a real humanist who usually made a lot of sense and whom I have liked to quote on *my* side.

literature
under attack

The major claim for literature, in the words of Denys Thompson, is that "it stands for humanity at a time when the human values are not upheld, as they used to be by religion and the home . . . or by education." The reading of great writing, it is alleged, can help the individual maintain his equilibrium, his sanity, and his sense of personal identity in a world fraught with chaos and confusion. Certainly many readers would agree that these and other virtues, such as the sheer pleasure afforded by reading, can help mankind keep in touch with humane values.

Before the nineteenth century, though, few made such august claims for literature. But during the cultural and spiritual crises of the 1800s literature quickly moved into the vacuum left by the decline of religious and other institutions. The first "Lit" courses were offered by colleges in the United States just a century ago. Shortly thereafter Harvard and other schools began to impose mandatory English composition and literature courses, often at the expense of classical languages and theology. By 1970 there were more than 70,000 English and humanities teachers in American universities, the largest faculty block in higher education.

Accompanying this spectacular growth was the rise of a number of prestigious schools of critical and interpretative thought—such as those led by I. A. Richards, T. S. Eliot, F. R. Leavis, Alan Tate, John Crowe Ransom, R. S. Crane, René Wellek, William Wimsatt, Austin Warren, Cleanth Brooks, William Empson, Northrop Frye—whose purpose was to determine what literature was (and what it was not), identify literary traditions, establish aesthetic norms and critical practice, ferret out symbolic patterns, and expose the "hidden gods" buried in ostensibly secular writings. Though many practitioners would deny it, the importance granted to literature by these schools of criticism was akin to that which once belonged to religion.

Today the quasi-religious assumptions about the role of literature in life are attacked from many sides. Even the assertion that there is a body of writing that can be labeled "literature" is dismissed as unprovable or outright sham, despite the thousands of essays churned out each year telling us what "literature" is and how it supposedly functions. The claim of some critics that only those writings which meet certain verifiable aesthetic standards can qualify as "literature" is likewise dismissed as nothing but cultural snobbery. "Culture," wrote Simone Weil, "is an instrument wielded by professors in order to produce professors who in their turn will produce professors."

Richard Poirier has written an essay, "What is English Studies, and If You Know What That Is, What Is English English Literature?," in which he claims there is "little evidence . . . that people of conventionally achieved literary culture or people who produce literature are any better at 'the exploration of life's problems' than are some, and not a few, who cannot read or write. Those who write simply ask us to take their language in one rather than in some other form. The form itself does not make them necessarily better or worse with respect to life." Some brilliant writers (like Céline) had no apparent difficulty collaborating with the Nazis because they were writers; nor is there any proof that reading the great books makes one more "civilized" than nonreaders.

Important modern writers have themselves charged that writing is a process which obscures truth, as Ionesco records in the excerpts from *Fragments of a Journal* included in this volume. And in his manifesto, "No More Masterpieces," Antonin Artaud charged that a written text, even one by Shakespeare, destroys the freedom and vitality of theatre.

For Professor Louis Kampf of M.I.T., the problem is less with the inhibiting presence of "masterpieces" than it is with the abuses made of literature and the literary tradition—abuses that reflect the same connection between literacy and human exploitation feared by Lévi-Strauss in " 'Civilized' Peoples and 'Primitive' Peoples." But now the symbols of manipulation are not administrative records but "great books" themselves, the "spiritual" component of literate society. In the universities, Kampf believes, the humanistic tradition is used to brainwash armies of future corporate functionaries into believing that their bureaucratic tasks are meaningfully related to the past. The ultimate goal of this process is "to make the acculturating mechanisms" of the society "more efficient."

In short the concept of "literature" is accused of lacking artistic meaning, of encouraging cultural elitism, of maintaining a professorial bureaucracy whose members perpetuate a mystique of literature to serve their own ends, of irrelevance to the social and ideological needs of the time and to the backgrounds of most third-world and lower-class white students, and of serving merely as a manipulative device to impose "acculturation" on future bureaucrats.

René Wellek, in "The Attack on Literature" provides a vigorous refutation of these charges. An outstanding literary scholar of the old school, Wellek believes that the concept of "literature" is valid; and that literature has been, and will continue to be, a positive force in human affairs.

The extent to which writers can overcome the problems raised by the contributors to this section will unquestionably determine the future of literacy as a cultural force. While, as Part Three shows, the purely functional uses of literacy are likely to survive in conjunction with other media, such is not the case with its "aesthetic" uses—insofar as the two can any longer be separated. The most important challenge to literacy is the development of its capacity to communicate the kinds of imaginative insights that will assist in the struggle for humane behavior. At present it is not at all clear, despite the optimistic tone of Wellek's last paragraphs, how this is likely to occur.

Chapter 9

excerpts from
"fragments of a journal"

Eugène Ionesco

To stop thinking, to make one's mind a blank: alas, animals think too, they, too, know fear, they are afraid of death. One cannot feel hunger and thirst. Why were we created?

I ought to have embarked long ago on this stubborn quest for knowledge and self-knowledge. If I'd set about it in time, I might have achieved something. Instead of writing literature! What a waste of time; I thought I had all of life ahead of me. Now time is pressing, the end is near, and haste is not favourable to my quest; indeed, it's because of literature that I can no longer understand anything at all. It's as though by writing books I had worn out all symbols without getting to the heart of them. They no longer speak to me with living voices. Words have killed images or concealed them. A civilization based on words is a lost civilization. Words create confusion. Words are not speech.

But these words were like masks, or else like dead leaves fallen to the ground. The tree of life and death is still there, bare and black. Nothing now can mask the deepest, most incurable distress. I am face to face with truth. . . .

I am constantly relapsing into literature. The fact of having been able to describe . . . images, of having put them into words more or less satisfactorily, flatters my vanity. I reflect that it may be well written. It may give pleasure to readers or critics. I say this, I tell myself this and then I relapse into literature. The fact of being conscious of

"Excerpts from *Fragments of a Journal*." From Eugène Ionesco, *Fragments of a Journal* (New York: Grove Press, Inc., 1969), pp. 61, 69, 72, 73, 89, 90, and 100. Reprinted by permission of Grove Press, Inc. and Faber and Faber Limited.

it does not save me. The fact of being conscious that I am conscious of literary values only makes things worse. I have to make a choice, though: vanity, the road to failure, or the other thing. One's not always lucky enough to get the knock-out blow, one's not always lucky enough to be desperate about life; I forget it, I seek consolation and amusement, I enjoy myself, I write my "private diary." I have tremendous vitality; nothing can exhaust it. Only dreams or nightmares can keep one awake. And yet it seems to me that some of the previous pages had nothing to do with words and writing. If I've relapsed into "literature," is it because the Administrator of the Comédie Française has just rung me up from Paris to tell me he's interested in my latest play? It doesn't take much to restore my unbalance. Let's eat an apple. . . .

It can't be said that art is devoid of all spiritual value. The artist is, after all, superior to the average man, the technician, the politician, anyone who is wholly unconscious. And yet he doesn't amount to very much. Arthur Rimbaud may have written *Les Illuminations,* people may declare that he was a visionary, but I don't believe in his visions nor in any other literary visions. I don't for one second believe in his illuminations. Art brings a tiny gleam, a tiny greyish gleam, a tiny hint of illumination, swamped in garrulousness.

Of course, words say nothing, if I may express myself thus: at most, an unexpected gesture, an image, an incident, a word come from nobody knows where may propel one into the unutterable experience. Whether I express myself with precision or without, whether my metaphors are apt or inadequate, lost in a flood of confused and rambling verbiage, it doesn't matter; in any case the deepest meaning is lost in explanations. There are no words for the deepest experience. The more I explain myself, the less I understand myself. Of course not everything is beyond the reach of words; but the living truth is. Words only say exactly what can be said, which has been known for a long time. Admitted; and not only admitted but also disputed, considered as inadmissible. But if it's been known for a long time and repeated so often, and we're still no further on, it means that I am right.

A single word can put you on the right track, a second disturbs you, and at the third you panic. With the fourth, utter confusion reigns. The *logos* once meant action as well; it has become paralysis. What's a word? Whatever is not lived with ardent intensity. When I say: is life worth dying for? I am still using words. But at least they're comic. Everyone must have noticed how much talk about language we get from young men from the Sorbonne and the Ecole Normale, from distinguished essayists and journalists, speechifyers and other progressive and wealthy intellectuals. It's become an obsession with them, a mania. If people talk so much about language it's because they're obsessed with what they lack. In the days of the Tower of Babel there must have been a great deal of talk about language too. Almost as much as today. The Word has become verbiage. Everyone has his word to say.

Words no longer demonstrate: they chatter. Words are literary. They are an escape. They stop silence from speaking. They deafen you. Instead of being action, they comfort you as best they can for your inaction. Words wear out thought, they impair it. Silence is golden. It ought to serve as guarantee for speech. Alas, we've got inflation. That, again, is just another word. What a civilization! No sooner do my anxieties withdraw a little than I start talking instead of trying to grasp reality, my reality, the realities, and words cease to be an instrument of search; I know nothing at all; and yet I teach. I've got a word or two to say, too. . . .

I demand the right to settle matters with myself. To be face to face with myself. Perhaps from my confrontation with myself something else may emerge. "Don't change, don't let all this anxiety rise to the surface, close your eyes, you wouldn't be able to endure it." But in any case I can't endure myself, it's time for me to become aware of things. It's time to assert myself. What's the good of struggling, says the other voice, what's the good? But I'm crippled, I'm choking, I'm dying because I cannot die, I cannot know. If I could only consider myself as already dead, my anguish would have died too. Consider myself as dead? I shan't succeed in doing that until death has killed me. I know, I know, it's better to kill oneself than to let oneself be killed. It seems to me an inaccessible mountain peak. And since I think it's impossible, it's no use my thinking of it any longer, it's nothing but literature. The world of literature, the impotent world, the world of partial lucidity, between strength and weakness. We should seek action, which means forgetfulness; or supreme lucidity, which is religion. There is no escape through literature; action, at least, provides that. I lament my impotence, I know what my sickness is, I describe it; I cannot reach its deepest source. As soon as I say to myself that these pages may perhaps be published, their truth is corrupted. They become counterfeit coins. Such introspection is valueless, sterile, harmful. It is not the knowledge that leads to the right path, the path that brings one out into the light. . . .

Chapter 10

no more masterpieces

Antonin Artaud

One of the reasons for the asphyxiating atmosphere in which we live without possible escape or remedy—and in which we all share, even the most revolutionary among us—is our respect for what has been written, formulated, or painted, what has been given form, as if all expression were not at last exhausted, were not at a point where things must break apart if they are to start anew and begin fresh.

We must have done with this idea of masterpieces reserved for a self-styled elite and not understood by the general public; the mind has no such restricted districts as those so often used for clandestine sexual encounters.

Masterpieces of the past are good for the past: they are not good for us. We have the right to say what has been said and even what has not been said in a way that belongs to us, a way that is immediate and direct, corresponding to present modes of feeling, and understandable to everyone.

It is idiotic to reproach the masses for having no sense of the sublime, when the sublime is confused with one or another of its formal manifestations, which are moreover always defunct manifestations. And if for example a contemporary public does not understand *Oedipus Rex*, I shall make bold to say that it is the fault of *Oedipus Rex* and not of the public.

In *Oedipus Rex* there is the theme of incest and the idea that nature mocks at morality and that there are certain unspecified powers

"No More Masterpieces." From Antonin Artaud, *The Theater and Its Double* (New York: Grove Press, Inc., 1958), pp. 74–83. Reprinted by permission of Grove Press, Inc. and Calder and Boyars Ltd. First published in 1938.

at large which we would do well to beware of, call them *destiny* or
anything you choose.

There is in addition the presence of a plague epidemic which is
a physical incarnation of these powers. But the whole in a manner and
language that have lost all touch with the rude and epileptic rhythm
of our time. Sophocles speaks grandly perhaps, but in a style that is
no longer timely. His language is too refined for this age, it is as if
he were speaking beside the point.

However, a public that shudders at train wrecks, that is familiar
with earthquakes, plagues, revolutions, wars; that is sensitive to the
disordered anguish of love, can be affected by all these grand notions
and asks only to become aware of them, but on condition that it is addressed in its own language, and that its knowledge of these things
does not come to it through adulterated trappings and speech that belong to extinct eras which will never live again.

Today as yesterday, the public is greedy for mystery: it asks only
to become aware of the laws according to which destiny manifests itself, and to divine perhaps the secret of its apparitions.

Let us leave textual criticism to graduate students, formal criticism to esthetes, and recognize that what has been said is not still to
be said; that an expression does not have the same value twice, does
not live two lives; that all words, once spoken, are dead and function
only at the moment when they are uttered, that a form, once it has
served, cannot be used again and asks only to be replaced by another,
and that the theater is the only place in the world where a gesture,
once made, can never be made the same way twice.

If the public does not frequent our literary masterpieces, it is
because those masterpieces are literary, that is to say, fixed; and fixed
in forms that no longer respond to the needs of the time.

Far from blaming the public, we ought to blame the formal
screen we interpose between ourselves and the public, and this new
form of idolatry, the idolatry of fixed masterpieces which is one of
the aspects of bourgeois conformism.

This conformism makes us confuse sublimity, ideas, and things
with the forms they have taken in time and in our minds—in our
snobbish, precious, aesthetic mentalities which the public does not
understand.

How pointless in such matters to accuse the public of bad taste
because it relishes insanities, so long as the public is not shown a
valid spectacle; and I defy anyone to show me *here* a spectacle valid
—valid in the supreme sense of the theater—since the last great romantic melodramas, i.e., since a hundred years ago.

The public, which takes the false for the true, has the sense of the true and always responds to it when it is manifested. However it is not upon the stage that the true is to be sought nowadays, but in the street; and if the crowd in the street is offered an occasion to show its human dignity, it will always do so.

If people are out of the habit of going to the theater, if we have all finally come to think of theater as an inferior art, a means of popular distraction, and to use it as an outlet for our worst instincts, it is because we have learned too well what the theater has been, namely, falsehood and illusion. It is because we have been accustomed for four hundred years, that is since the Renaissance, to a purely descriptive and narrative theater—storytelling psychology; it is because every possible ingenuity has been exerted in bringing to life on the stage plausible but detached beings, with the spectacle on one side, the public on the other—and because the public is no longer shown anything but the mirror of itself.

Shakespeare himself is responsible for this aberration and decline, this disinterested idea of the theater which wishes a theatrical performance to leave the public intact, without setting off one image that will shake the organism to its foundations and leave an ineffaceable scar.

If, in Shakespeare, a man is sometimes preoccupied with what transcends him, it is always in order to determine the ultimate consequences of this preoccupation within him, i.e., psychology.

Psychology, which works relentlessly to reduce the unknown to the known, to the quotidian and the ordinary, is the cause of the theater's abasement and its fearful loss of energy, which seems to me to have reached its lowest point. And I think both the theater and we ourselves have had enough of psychology.

I believe furthermore that we can all agree on this matter sufficiently so that there is no need to descend to the repugnant level of the modern and French theater to condemn the theater of psychology.

Stories about money, worry over money, social careerism, the pangs of love unspoiled by altruism, sexuality sugarcoated with an eroticism that has lost its mystery have nothing to do with the theater, even if they do belong to psychology. These torments, seductions, and lusts before which we are nothing but Peeping Toms gratifying our cravings, tend to go bad, and their rot turns to revolution: we must take this into account.

But this is not our most serious concern.

If Shakespeare and his imitators have gradually insinuated the idea of art for art's sake, with art on one side and life on the other, we can rest on this feeble and lazy idea only as long as the life outside endures. But there are too many signs that everything that used to sustain our lives no longer does so, that we are all mad, desperate, and sick. And I call for *us* to react.

This idea of a detached art, of poetry as a charm which exists only to distract our leisure, is a decadent idea and an unmistakable symptom of our power to castrate.

Our literary admiration for Rimbaud, Jarry, Lautréamont, and a few others, which has driven two men to suicide, but turned into café gossip for the rest, belongs to this idea of literary poetry, of detached art, of neutral spiritual activity which creates nothing and produces nothing; and I can bear witness that at the very moment when that kind of personal poetry which involves only the man who creates it and only at the moment he creates it broke out in its most abusive fashion, the theater was scorned more than ever before by poets who have never had the sense of direct and concerted action, nor of efficacity, nor of danger.

We must get rid of our superstitious valuation of texts and *written* poetry. Written poetry is worth reading once, and then should be destroyed. Let the dead poets make way for others. Then we might even come to see that it is our veneration for what has already been created, however beautiful and valid it may be, that petrifies us, deadens our responses, and prevents us from making contact with that underlying power, call it thought-energy, the life force, the determinism of change, lunar menses, or anything you like. Beneath the poetry of the texts, there is the actual poetry, without form and without text. And just as the efficacity of masks in the magic practices of certain tribes is exhausted—and these masks are no longer good for anything except museums—so the poetic efficacity of a text is exhausted; yet the poetry and the efficacity of the theater are exhausted least quickly of all, since they permit the *action* of what is gesticulated and pronounced, and which is never made the same way twice.

It is a question of knowing what we want. If we are prepared for war, plague, famine, and slaughter we do not even need to say so, we have only to continue as we are; continue behaving like snobs, rushing en masse to hear such and such a singer, to see such and such an admirable performance which never transcends the realm of art (and even the Russian ballet at the height of its splendor never transcended the realm of art), to marvel at such and such an exhibition of painting in which exciting shapes explode here and there but at random and without any genuine consciousness of the forces they could rouse.

This empiricism, randomness, individualism, and anarchy must cease.

Enough of personal poems, benefitting those who create them much more than those who read them.

Once and for all, enough of this closed, egoistic, and personal art.

Our spiritual anarchy and intellectual disorder is a function of the anarchy of everything else—or rather, everything else is a function of this anarchy.

I am not one of those who believe that civilization has to change in order for the theater to change; but I do believe that the theater, utilized in the highest and most difficult sense possible, has the power to influence the aspect and formation of things: and the encounter upon the stage of two passionate manifestations, two living centers, two nervous magnetisms is something as entire, true, even decisive, as, in life, the encounter of one epidermis with another in a timeless debauchery.

That is why I propose a theater of cruelty.—With this mania we all have for depreciating everything, as soon as I have said "cruelty," everybody will at once take it to mean "blood." But *"theater of cruelty"* means a theater difficult and cruel for myself first of all. And, on the level of performance, it is not the cruelty we can exercise upon each other by hacking at each other's bodies, carving up our personal anatomies, or, like Assyrian emperors, sending parcels of human ears, noses, or neatly detached nostrils through the mail, but the much more terrible and necessary cruelty which things can exercise against us. We are not free. And the sky can still fall on our heads. And the theater has been created to teach us that first of all.

Either we will be capable of returning by present-day means to this superior idea of poetry and poetry-through-theater which underlies the Myths told by the great ancient tragedians, capable once more of entertaining a religious idea of the theater (without meditation, useless contemplation, and vague dreams), capable of attaining awareness and a possession of certain dominant forces, of certain notions that control all others, and (since ideas, when they are effective, carry their energy with them) capable of recovering within ourselves those energies which ultimately create order and increase the value of life, or else we might as well abandon ourselves now, without protest, and recognize that we are no longer good for anything but disorder, famine, blood, war, and epidemics.

Either we restore all the arts to a central attitude and necessity, finding an analogy between a gesture made in painting or the theater, and a gesture made by lava in a volcanic explosion, or we must stop painting, babbling, writing, or doing whatever it is we do.

I propose to bring back into the theater this elementary magical idea, taken up by modern psychoanalysis, which consists in effecting a patient's cure by making him assume the apparent and exterior attitudes of the desired condition.

I propose to renounce our empiricism of imagery, in which the unconscious furnishes images at random, and which the poet arranges at random too, calling them poetic and hence hermetic images, as if the kind of trance that poetry provides did not have its reverberations throughout the whole sensibility, in every nerve, and as if poetry were some vague force whose movements were invariable.

I propose to return through the theater to an idea of the physical knowledge of images and the means of inducing trances, as in Chinese medicine which knows, over the entire extent of the human anatomy, at what points to puncture in order to regulate the subtlest functions.

Those who have forgotten the communicative power and magical mimesis of a gesture, the theater can reinstruct, because a gesture carries its energy with it, and there are still human beings in the theater to manifest the force of the gesture made.

To create art is to deprive a gesture of its reverberation in the organism, whereas this reverberation, if the gesture is made in the conditions and with the force required, incites the organism and, through it, the entire individuality, to take attitudes in harmony with the gesture.

The theater is the only place in the world, the last general means we still possess of directly affecting the organism and, in periods of neurosis and petty sensuality like the one in which we are immersed, of attacking this sensuality by physical means it cannot withstand.

If music affects snakes, it is not on account of the spiritual notions it offers them, but because snakes are long and coil their length upon the earth, because their bodies touch the earth at almost every point; and because the musical vibrations which are communicated to the earth affect them like a very subtle, very long massage; and I propose to treat the spectators like the snakecharmer's subjects and conduct them *by means of their organisms* to an apprehension of the subtlest notions.

At first by crude means, which will gradually be refined. These immediate crude means will hold their attention at the start.

That is why in the "theater of cruelty" the spectator is in the center and the spectacle surrounds him.

In this spectacle the sonorisation is constant: sounds, noises, cries are chosen first for their vibratory quality, then for what they represent.

Among these gradually refined means light is interposed in its turn. Light which is not created merely to add color or to brighten, and which brings its power, influence, suggestions with it. And the light of a green cavern does not sensually dispose the organism like the light of a windy day.

After sound and light there is action, and the dynamism of action: here the theater, far from copying life, puts itself whenever possible in communication with pure forces. And whether you accept or deny them, there is nevertheless a way of speaking which gives the name of "forces" to whatever brings to birth images of energy in the unconscious, and gratuitous crime on the surface.

A violent and concentrated action is a kind of lyricism: it summons up supernatural images, a bloodstream of images, a bleeding spurt of images in the poet's head and in the spectator's as well.

Whatever the conflicts that haunt the mind of a given period, I defy any spectator to whom such violent scenes will have transferred their blood, who will have felt in himself the transit of a superior action, who will have seen the extraordinary and essential movements of his thought illuminated in extraordinary deeds—the violence and blood having been placed at the service of the violence of the thought —I defy that spectator to give himself up, once outside the theater, to ideas of war, riot, and blatant murder.

So expressed, this idea seems dangerous and sophomoric. It will be claimed that example breeds example, that if the attitude of cure induces cure, the attitude of murder will induce murder. Everything depends upon the manner and the purity with which the thing is done. There is a risk. But let it not be forgotten that though a theatrical gesture is violent, it is disinterested; and that the theater teaches precisely the uselessness of the action which, once done, is not to be done, and the superior use of the state unused by the action and which, *restored,* produces a purification.

I propose then a theater in which violent physical images crush and hypnotize the sensibility of the spectator seized by the theater as by a whirlwind of higher forces.

A theater which, abandoning psychology, recounts the extraordinary, stages natural conflicts, natural and subtle forces, and presents itself first of all as an exceptional power of redirection. A theater that induces trance, as the dances of Dervishes induce trance, and that addresses itself to the organism by precise instruments, by the same means as those of certain tribal music cures which we admire on records but are incapable of originating among ourselves.

There is a risk involved, but in the present circumstances I believe it is a risk worth running. I do not believe we have managed to revitalize the world we live in, and I do not believe it is worth the trouble of clinging to; but I do propose something to get us out of our marasmus, instead of continuing to complain about it, and about the boredom, inertia, and stupidity of everything.

Chapter 11

the humanities and inhumanities

Louis Kampf

American higher education, like any institution, lives by myths. Still feeling threatened by the seriousness of purpose shown by students during last spring's campus rebellions, the educator's myth of the moment informs us of both the practicality and the transcendent beauty of a liberal (or humanistic) education. The same noble speech is being (or has recently been) addressed to thousands of freshmen: whether at West Point, Swarthmore, the Texas College of Mines, M.I.T. or the University of Michigan hardly seems to matter. It informs them of the primacy of a liberal—rather than a specialized, or technical—education. The humanities, the speech continues, release us from irrationally held prejudices; they open our minds; they teach us to be generalists instead of specialists. In short, a liberal education transforms the narrow career-oriented youth into a free, though of course responsible, man or woman of culture.

The underlying assumption of the speech is that four years of exposure to a balanced curriculum will produce young men and women who are objective, rational, yet not without feeling; who being free of ideological blinders will be blessed with a sense of their own autonomy. Having been made intellectually independent by their study of Homer, the Renaissance, atomic particles, Wordsworth, brain waves, Pop art and total environments, they are capable of discovering the relevant past and applying it to the problems of the moment. They are prisoners neither of history nor of the imperatives of current urgencies. Consequently they are eminently capable of dealing with the

"The Humanities and Inhumanities." From Louis Kampf, "The Humanities and Inhumanities," *The Nation*, September 30, 1968, pp. 309–13. Reprinted by permission of the publisher.

insistent pressures of change. Having absorbed the best civilization has to offer, they will be able to retain their humanity though practically engulfed by inhuman events. Briefly put, they will be liberal. Certainly, they will not resort to the barbarism of riots.

I suppose there is a grain of truth at the center of this hollow rhetoric. Certainly the motives which generate such words are often decent enough. Yet I suspect that the hearts of most academics attending freshman orientation sink as they hear the noble sentiments being piled on. There is a moment when one expects the dean of freshmen either to burst into tears, to choke on his own words, or perhaps to double up with laughter. He knows that his colleagues know his words are fake; and I suspect that most of the students see us all—teachers, deans, administrators—for the frauds we are. Is it not time we forgot about the nobility of the humanities and asked what their real function is, what social purposes they, in fact, serve?

Hardly a day passes without some representative of the industrial elite letting us know that America's corporate enterprises, not to speak of its government agencies, need managers who are not only steeped in the techniques of operations research but who are equally adept at quoting John Donne or T. S. Eliot. At M.I.T., the Sloan Fellows in Industrial Management are expected to devote a fairly substantial amount of their time to the study of literature. The exposure to literature, we are to assume, makes them better—indeed, more enlightened —managers. But who are these managers? What is their task?

> No one knows who will live in this cage in the future, or whether at the end of this tremendous development entirely new prophets will arise, or there will be a great rebirth of old ideas and ideals, or, if neither, mechanized petrification, embellished with a sort of convulsive self-importance. For the last stage of this cultural development, it might well be truly said: "Specialists without spirit, sensualists without hearts; this nullity imagines that it has attained a level of civilization never before achieved."

The melancholy words are Max Weber's. The occupants of his cage are the functionaries of the bureaucracy bequeathed us by the Protestant ethic and the spirit of capitalism. The culture he feared was one in which rationalization of the profit motive, rather than the simple urge to earn money, becomes its own end, and efficiency is pursued with religious—yet mechanical—zeal. To further such ends, traditional education is replaced by training programs for technicians and efficiency experts. M.I.T., the Harvard Business School, and their brothers and sisters were fathered by the needs of industrial capitalism.

But today such an analysis may seem naive, even simple-minded. We know that our business schools give courses in social responsibility; moreover, our industrial managers conduct seminars on the needs of the Third World and the family structure of the poor. And who would doubt that this derives from anything but the best of motives? But before we congratulate ourselves on our good luck, we might take a closer look at modern capitalism. Clearly we have moved beyond that stage of rationalization which merely involves problems in engineering. Moreover, the complexities of modern finance—the mother of industrial development—involve a subtlety of human manipulation undreamed of by Weber's contemporaries. And as the complexity insinuates itself into all areas of the social system, we reach a point where our corporations and financial institutions effectively control most public—as well as private—institutions. As Kenneth Galbraith has pointed out, in this situation the main function of the American Government is not to promote the public sector but to keep the social order stable enough for business to do its business. Its second large task is to see that America's educational institutions provide the corporate machine with enough functionaries to keep it oiled.

The function of higher education, then, is to turn out those industrial cadres, rocket engineers, researchers, planners, personnel managers and development experts needed by the economy. But not only this: our colleges and universities have also been charged with the task of shaping the more ordinary functionaries: the kind who were once not subject to a four-year grind through the educational mill. Looked at in terms of real industrial need these four years of classes, laboratories, football games, hours in the library and bull sessions seem entirely superfluous. But that is not the point. For beyond immediate mechanical requirements there are the larger social imperatives. Social order must be maintained, and the whole fabric of traditions which gives a society its continuity must be kept intact. If this proves to be impossible, then at least appearances must be kept up; patches covering up the rents must be made invisible. As ordinary mechanical tasks multiply, as more of the labor force takes on white-collar jobs and finds itself pushed into the middle-class, the process of acculturation becomes increasingly difficult. Formerly, those few who climbed the social ladder learned their manners—were educated to the proper social style—by their gradual exposure to the more or less culturally advanced. This was a slow and haphazard process; many fell by the wayside and never attained the style of life appropriate to their economic station. If the production of consumer goods is to expand, the goods must be consumed. To accomplish this, the new industrial cadres must be prepared for an "enriched"—that is, a cultured—style of life. Above all, the new class must never be allowed to feel that it constitutes a new industrial proletariat.

Let me return to Weber's metaphor: the animals in the bureaucratic cage must be civilized. Yet having consciousness, the task of civilizing tends to go beyond the development of conditioned reflexes. It must concern itself with the inescapable fact of human creativity and with the reality of man's historical memory. Both are, after all, basic components of what we call culture; they are integral to man as a species. The ordinary functionary, then, must be convinced that the rationalized task he performs—his ordinary, and inexplicable, job of work—is somehow connected to traditional culture—to all those monuments, both artistic and social, which represent our historical aspirations. What had formerly been the property of an elite now also belongs to the bureaucrat; for he, after all, has become a member of that elite. Or so he thinks. In any case, he knows he has his place in the traditions of the social system—and it is good. Consequently, there is no point in directing the anger of one's frustrations, of one's secret dissatisfactions, at the system itself, for one would be turning them against oneself—against that historic culture one has attained.

And therefore the future home economist, insurance salesman, even department store floorwalker must be made to believe that these tasks are—however mysteriously—connected to Homer, the Athenians, the Judeo-Christian tradition, and the rest of our cultural baggage. The connections may not be clear, but we feel a terrible guilt if we do not perceive them.

To perform this job of acculturation requires an expanding system of colleges and universities; to run them, a force of educational functionaries whose size seems to have no limit. The opportunities for administrators, professors, research executives, even writers, painters and composers are getting better every day. If nothing else, our colleges provide a marvelous haven for Cabinet members, mayors, Presidential advisers and generals, who are temporarily out of work. They, like their fellow humanities professors, are also students of the liberal arts. But, once more, this job of training and acculturation must proceed without upsetting our traditional notion of the university's function. The educational cadres must believe that they perform the humane tasks of scholarship. So they all write articles, and monographs, and books, and reviews of books and bibliographies of these reviews. At the highest level, in our important graduate schools, they train people like themselves to train people like themselves, to train people like themselves, to train people like themselves. . . .

Far from teaching young people to become aware of their capacities, a liberal education allows them—worst, forces them—to ignore themselves. As for the nagging reality of a world desperately in need of social change, the ordinary liberal education pretends either that the need does not exist, or that it can be taken care of painlessly, as a matter of ordinary academic routine. One thing is certain: change must do no violence to the traditional humanistic values embedded in the curriculum. These foundations of a liberal education are sacred. Thus the master task of the humanities becomes one of accommodating students to the social dislocations of industrial society by hiding their painful apprenticeship—their rite of admission to an appropriate office—behind the mask of a traditional culture. Confronted by the radical transformation of roles played by the educated, the liberal arts must assure us that the *status quo* is, after all, being maintained.

An odd development. Matthew Arnold once taught us that the object of studying the best that had been thought or said is to criticize our present mode of life, to make us see the object as it really is. Instead the study of our classics seems to provide us with ideological blinders. It mystifies—to use R. D. Laing's phrase—the very basis of our experience: our way of seeing, feeling, knowing. The humanities have been the educational system's unwitting collaborators in destroying our experience—that is, our humanity. For by blinding us to social mechanisms they have made us unconscious; they have made us the victims of a myth; they have kept us from seeing things as they really are. And, to quote Laing again, "If our experience is destroyed, our behavior will be destructive." And so it is. It is so because our culture has taught us to disguise competitive aggression as social benevolence, oppression as freedom, hate as love. These marvelous transformations have been effected not only by those who control our most powerful institutions but by our educators—our experts in acculturation. The lesson concerning the relationship of culture to aggression taught us by *Civilization and Its Discontents* seems not to have sunk in. Or perhaps it has sunk in all too well. As Freud observed, we desperately stand in need of our defense mechanisms.

But perhaps we are running out of defense mechanisms. Perhaps the contradictions liberal education creates for students are beginning to turn on us; perhaps the young will make us ask those questions we have so long refused to ask.

How so? The meaning of life is in action—whether the acts be physical or mental. Fulfilled action frees us; it makes us independent. When we can relate our thoughts, our yearnings, to activity: when our vague projections issue in conscious work—then we may rightly feel that we have our lives under a measure of control. Formerly the purpose of a traditional liberal education had been to train a cultured —and humane—elite. The act of ruling, of governing and giving guidance, was the activity which gave life its meaning; it fulfilled the objectives of the education. Clearly we still have the same goals in mind for the liberal arts today. Supposedly they teach us to be creative and to act humanely. And are these not the standards we set for our elite? But consciousness has made a fool of our objectives; for the young—or at least for some of them—the ideological fog has been cleared by the very contradictions of their education.

Precisely because we have been liberal in our education, our best students have come to understand that their deepest intellectual concerns—their very enthusiasms, their most intense involvements—cannot issue in any sort of activity which makes a claim to any social relevance beyond acculturation. And if there be no such social relevance, how can activity be fulfilling? Thus there is an almost inevitable split between thought and action. Thought may be free, but activity is controlled; stated educational objectives may be ethical, but actions immoral. The thoughts and feelings engendered by liberal education —the cultural enrichment we offer the young—become ideological masks for the politics of those who rule.

And the best of our students know this. They know that their studies are divorced from meaningful activity. They know that their courses are not intended to further their self-development: rather they become a part of the students' property, their capital. Their knowledge —technical or humanistic—makes them a product. As the material and cultural embodiments of this knowledge grow—and recall, these embodiments are products of man's self-formation, actualizations of his ideas—our practical activities, in a most ironic fashion, become ever more faintly related to our thoughts and feelings: their connection to the meaningful development of ideas and passions becomes more and more tenuous. Consciousness has once more played us for the destructive fools we are. For the object of a liberal education, we tell ourselves, is the fulfillment of individual capacities, of ideas and passions. Through such fulfillment, we assume, men can become whole, sane, peaceful and free—that is, humane.

But the split we have created in the student's life has allowed him to see his education for what it is. He knows that his studies— especially those in the humanities, he is informed by our managers —make him a more valuable piece of private property. He knows that his labor in the classroom transforms him into an object; that he makes of himself a product.

Since it is the student himself who becomes the product of his own labor, he is in tension with himself; he is split. He sells those treasures which, we have taught him, best represent his humanity— that is, his civilization, his culture, his liberal education. And so he is at war with his own being, for the battle over this piece of private property is a battle over himself. For the best of our students the study of the humanities creates a more intense consciousness of this situation. Indeed, self-knowledge creates a condition which puts that very education—the act of preparing oneself for one's role—beyond endurance. What truly liberally educated human being can bear to be a commodity with consciousness?

Such are the ends of a liberal education—or at least one of the unintended ends. In their attempt to use the traditional liberal arts to gain social consent, our managers have created a situation where students must risk their sanity in order to enact the lessons of their education; or they must turn into commodities, accommodating themselves—consciously or otherwise—to the lie on which their education is based.

In seeking alternatives, the educator's first impulse is to suggest curricular reform: jiggle the mechanism a bit, make a great-books course out of freshman composition, even have them reading Norman Mailer and Mao Tse-tung. Such reforms, we assume, will effect a fundamental change in the lives of our students. I doubt it. Changes in the curriculum—though often valuable and necessary—may have the ultimate effect of making the acculturating mechanisms more efficient. They may make the beast more cultured, but will not change its objectives. To break out of Weber's cage, to face the imperatives of fundamental change without dogma—if these are the conditions to which we hope our students will aspire, we shall need a most fundamental critique of the very social basis and function of higher education. Much academic political science will serve as an example. Aside from its more gross involvements with the CIA, the field's major object is to put government *policy*—unlike the more trivial matter of its *execution*—beyond criticism: to harden ideologies like the "national interest" into unassailable dogmas. Political science has done its job well, for it has succeeded in putting real political inquiry beyond the pale of academic respectability. This situation will not be changed by curricular reforms alone. If students are once more to ask meaningful questions about the state, and if they are to meet these questions with programs they can translate into action, the very *ends* we set for political science will have to be changed.

The objective of a liberal education, it seems to me, should be the harmonious reconciliation of philosophy (that is, our ways of thinking), action and nature (the world; what there is). This condition is possible only when we do not feel estranged from the products of our thoughts and actions, when we do not feel separated from the nature we have helped to create. Unhappily, industrial capitalism is rooted in these divisions, in our divided state philosophy (our principles of education) must not be allowed to become an integral expression of culture; it must not serve to rationalize the divisions induced by the industrial system. It can remain philosophy, rather than ideology, only as it is *critical*. And so for the humanities or liberal arts.

How is this criticism to be expressed? Most often, I suspect, in acts which appear irrational, if not deranged. On October 16, 1967, while watching nearly 300 students turning in their draft cards at Arlington Street Church in Boston, I understood—and was saddened by that understanding—that these young men were involved in a desperate act of rejecting a civilization. The moral outrage required for this heroic act is disfiguring; it warps one's sense of reality; it too makes one's view of the world partial. Yet this seemingly mad act of rejecting an illegitimate and immoral authority was really an attempt to relate thought to action; to assert that the products of one's actions are one's own; that freedom—or at least the struggle for it—is a human necessity. Saying "Hell, no, we won't go!" is one way for the student to expose the lie of his education. Exploiting the class privilege of one's college deferment is, after all, a moral fraud—a fraud to which higher education not only closes its eyes but which it encourages. Ironically, in their act of criticism, in their act of rejection in willfully separating themselves from society these draft resisters tried to assert their wholeness.

Yet what of the madness of this act? Recent studies of schizophrenics have shown that insanity may provide the morally sensitive with the only means of staying alive in a disordered world. The ordering principle imposed by insanity on destructive chaos keeps one from suicide. This is one way of relating thought to action; or, more simply, to *act*—rather than turning inward self-destructively. Yet there is an alternative to pathology. And the students who take their education seriously and resist the draft have pointed to that alternative. Our ordering principle as educators must be criticism or, going further, counteraction, resistance. This may not sound much like the detachment, the wholeness, we associate with the humanities. Indeed, we know criticism tends to induce disorder and most of its serious practitioners often act like uncivilized madmen. But consider that the only real choice may be whether to be mad (though civilized) on society's terms, or on one's own.

If resistance be madness, it is at least human madness, not the rationalized lunacy of an abstract process. If our students are to retain —or perhaps discover—their humanity, they will have to oppose the system of acculturation and spiritual servitude which our colleges encourage. And opposition to abstractions constantly tempts one into irrational confrontations: the bars of the cage are beyond rationality.

Surely, the truly humanistic educator must strive to create a world which does not demand of our students acts of madness as the price for spiritual wholeness. Our primary need then is not for a liberal education but for one which is actively committed to an end. If we are to break out of the empty rhetoric of liberal educational reform, scholarship may need to become allied with activism.

Activism on what front? Not on the campus alone. For one thing, the university is not the place where students and their teachers are most likely to liberate themselves from the shackles of ideology. For higher education's institutional nature has shaped it into an instrument of perpetuation for our most cherished—that is, humanistic—ideologies: the university and most of its faculty has a vested interest to protect. And if we are to take Richard Hofstadter's commencement address at Columbia as an index, that vested interest will be defended against campus activists in the name of free scholarly inquiry. For it is the student strikers, Professor Hofstadter would have us believe, who are the chief threat to the values of humane scholarship.

Those scholars concerned with liberating themselves from such academic dogma and effecting fundamental change in the role played by the liberal arts, might have to begin by forming political groupings (such as the New University Conference) which create alliances both within and outside the university. These groupings will have to gain a sense of identity by taking clear, strong and public stances on the most important moral issues which confront our students: Vietnam, the draft, race, poverty, the nature of higher education, the uses of scholarship. Or to go deeper: American imperialism, war itself, the function of private property, sex and aggression. What is more analyses should be complemented by meaningful political action. Such activity may, in some cases, involve divisions within the faculty. But this surely must be the first step if our philosophy is to relate to our acts. Some things cannot—and must not—be smoothed over. Surely one thing our students must learn is to take their thoughts seriously.

The special urgency and occasional violence of the students' demands for university reform derive, I think, from an intuition that the liberal arts, rather than being the property of educational establishments, should embody our civilization's highest achievements. This intuition makes the integration of the liberal arts into the students' daily lives a condition toward which they (and we) desperately yearn. Yet if we are to see the object as it is, in Matthew Arnold's sense, we must look at the liberal arts within their social context. If liberal education is to perform its proper function—to help the students see things as they are, to face them humanely and freely—then that education must be placed within an appropriate social context. Creating this context becomes, consequently, the foremost task for the liberal arts.

This involves a transformation of consciousness, a transformation which must be radical—that is, it must take hold at the root. To reach this goal, the economic and social conditions which enslave our students must also be radically transformed. Is this possible inside our educational institutions? Within the imperatives of our social system? I doubt it. Yet our society is being shaken; it changes radically in spite of ourselves, and in spite of our universities. Though we have no clear answers or directives for action, we must make the attempt. For only in the attempt will our analyses unfold, our activity become consciously meaningful.

Chapter 12

the attack on literature

René Wellek

In recent years we have heard much about the "death of literature," the "end of art," the "death of culture" and have become familiar with such terms as "antiart" and "postculture." We have been told by Jacques Ehrmann that "literature, a dumping ground of fine feelings, a museum of 'belles-lettres,' has had its day." Norman Mailer believes that "we have passed the point in civilization where we can ever look at anything as an art work."

I should like to examine the arguments for these views, to disentangle their motives and to set them in an historical perspective by tracing the term and the concept of "literature" through their history.

We can distinguish among several directions from which the attack on literature has come in recent decades.

One is politically motivated. It is the view that literature (and presumably all art) is conservative or at least a conserving power, which serves only the interests of the ruling class. To quote some examples, Roland Barthes, in France, has said that "literature is constitutionally reactionary"; in Germany, Oswald Wiener has complained that "the alphabet was imposed by higher-ups": and in this country, Louis Kampf, who was president of the Modern Language Association in 1971, has charged, in the Autumn, 1971, *New Literary History 3*, that "the very category of art has become one more instrument of making class distinctions." In "Notes Toward a Radical Culture" he asserts that the very concept of culture "is rooted in

From René Wellek, "The Attack on Literature," *The American Scholar*, 42, No. 1, Winter 1972/73. Copyright © 1973 by the United Chapters of Phi Beta Kappa. Reprinted by permission of the publishers.

social elitism." It can be "little else but an instrument of class oppression." "Initiating the underprivileged to the cultural treasures of the West could be a form of oppression—a weapon in the hands of those who rule" as "high culture tends to reinforce the given alignments of power within the society" (*Change*, May–June, 1970). The logical deduction from Kampf's argument would be that people should be denied access to great literature and art in the name of their political advancement. Louis Kampf describes himself standing on the Piazza Navona in Rome, admiring the baroque fountains and architecture but thinking rather of "the crimes, the human suffering, which made both the scene and my being there possible." "My being there" alludes presumably to the grant he received from a foundation or university to travel to Rome—money that he considers tainted because it is amassed by economic exploitation. He hates "the economic system which has invested finely chiseled stone with a price. Our esthetics are rooted in surplus value," he concludes, appealing to Marxist terminology but not, of course, rejecting the grant. In a different mood he recommends the destruction of what he considers a conspicuous symbol of high culture. "The movement should have harassed Lincoln Center from the beginning. Not a performance should go by without disruption. The fountains should be dried with calcium chloride, the statuary pissed on, the walls smeared with shit." These incitements to vandalism are printed on fine paper in a volume entitled *The New Left*.

No doubt, many splendid works of architecture were built with slave labor, beginning with the Egyptian pyramids, and the money that paid for the fountains on the Piazza Navona came, presumably, from the papal treasury, which collected taxes in ways we might consider unjust and oppressive. But the generalized rage against all art and literature seems, to say the least, most unjust toward large trends of literature in many lands. Even the briefest reflection will recall the eminently subversive, or at least liberalizing, role of literature in many historical situations: the French revolution was prepared by the *philosophes;* the Russian Revolution drew sustenance from a long line of writers critical of the Tsarist regime; the idea of a unified Italy was kept alive for centuries by her poets. The rebirth, in the nineteenth century, of the Greeks and the Hungarians, the Czechs and the Poles, was triggered by poets and men of letters, and today few would refuse admiration for his heroic resistance against new oppression to Alexander Solzhenitsyn or deny the prominent role of writers in the "Prague Spring" of 1968.

Thus the political attack on literature simply amounts to an attack on conservative ideology, which necessarily has been expressed in print, just as revolutionary ideology has found expression in print, struggling, no doubt, with the obstacles of censorship and government monopoly of print long before the advent of modern totalitarianism, right or left. As long ago as 1816 William Hazlitt complained, on the occasion of Shakespeare's *Coriolanus,* that "imagination is an aristocratic faculty," that "it is right royal, putting the one above the infinite many, might before right," that "the language of poetry naturally falls in with the language of power" and that "the principle of poetry is a very antileveling principle." Still, even in his time, Blake and Shelley showed that this is not necessarily true and that, as common sense tells us, literature and poetry as such cannot be guilty; men and writers say what they want to say—conservative or revolutionary thoughts, good or evil thoughts. The political attack on literature is a foolish generalization.

Much more serious and interesting is the attack on literature that is basically motivated by a distrust of language. Since the dawn of history many have felt that language fails to express their deepest emotions and insights, that the mystery of the universe or even of a flower eludes expression in language. Mystics have said so, in many variations, about their experience of the transcendent. Shakespeare has Othello say on meeting Desdemona again after landing on Cyprus: "I cannot speak enough of this content; it stops me here; it is too much of joy." Cordelia in answering Lear's fatal question can say only, "Nothing. . . . I cannot heave my heart into my mouth." Goethe constantly complains of the inadequacy of Language and the German Language in particular. Philosophers, at least since Locke, have formulated their suspicion of words, and Bishop Berkeley has exhorted us "to draw the curtain of words to behold the fairest tree of knowledge." Fritz Mauthner's three volume *Critique of Language* accumulates impressive evidence for this indictment; and the British analytical philosophers have made us more aware of the precariousness and shiftiness of our abstract and emotional vocabulary. The frightening inflation of the word in journalism and propaganda has brought home to a great many that the old certainties about terms such as "democracy," "justice" and "liberty" are gone forever. Linguists such as Benjamin Whorf have tried to show how closely grammatical and syntactical categories shape the view of the world of different people in different cultures; the Hopi Indians, he argued, see a very different order of the world from ours. Philosophers such as Ernst Cassirer, extending Kantian insights, have demonstrated that language builds the very structure of our knowledge. We all speak of the indescribable, the unspeakable, we say that words fail us, that words cannot express this horror or that beauty.

This old feeling has in the last century led to a definite rejection of normal language by poets struggling with elusive inner states of mind. Mallarmé was one of the first to despair of expressing the mystery of the universe, which he felt not only to be immensely dark but also hollow, empty and silent. Hugo von Hofmannsthal, in a fictitious letter of Lord Chandos to Bacon (1902), expressed his discontent with language, his (or rather his letter-writer's) justification for falling silent, because he wished only to "think with the heart." Today this motif has become insistent and almost commonplace. J. Hillis Miller tells us that "all literature is necessarily a sham. It captures in its subtle pages not the reality of darkness but its verbal image. . . . Words, the medium of fiction, are a fabrication of man's intellect. They are part of the human lie" (*Poets of Reality*). In France, Roland Barthes complains that "literature is a system of deceptive signification": it is "emphatically signifying, but never finally signified" (*Essais critiques*). The Saussurian terminology hides a simple thought: a word can never become a thing. Michel Foucault in *Les Mots et les Choses* has construed a whole history of the human mind in three stages of its attitude toward language. Before the advent of rationalism men assumed that words are things; they believed in the magic of words. In the Enlightenment people wanted to discover the order of things by words or, in Foucault's technical jargon, they wanted to find "a nomenclature which would be also a taxonomy." Our own period has concluded, as Foucault puts it, that "the thing being represented falls outside of the representation itself," and that man is thus unhappily trapped in a language game of which he knows nothing. There is no relation between language and reality. Language and literature have no cognitive value.

One result of this criticism of language has been the current cult of silence. Taken literally it lends itself to ridicule. In the nineteenth century one could laugh at Carlyle's gospel of silence in thirty volumes, and one might feel that there is nothing easier than to be silent. Still, George Steiner, Susan Sontag, Ihab Hassan and other advocates of silence continue writing. But silence, as Susan Sontag recognizes, has become a metaphor for "a perceptual and cultural clean slate," the end of art, the ultimate horror. Samuel Beckett in *Endgame* has been "looking for the voice of his silence." But Theodor Adorno's famous saying, "No poetry after Auschwitz," is not a practical solution. The artist's dissatisfaction with language can only be expressed by language. Pause may be a device to express the inexpressible but the pause cannot be prolonged indefinitely, cannot be simply silence as such. It needs a contrast, it needs a beginning and an end. Even John Cage in his notorious piece of music in which

three musicians or rather performers appeared and did nothing, had
to time it four minutes and thirty-three seconds; he could not have
kept it up for even four hours. Actually he replaced music by an act
of pantomime that aroused expectations he disappointed. He manipulated his audience and their time sense, put on a show, made a joke,
but made no music of silence since there is no silent poetry or literature.

In France, Maurice Blanchot has prophesied the "disappear-
ance of literature" and has envisaged "the death of the last writer."
He recalls that there have been ages and countries without writers,
and he dreams of ages without them in the future. He prophesies
that "a great disgust against books will seize us." The age without
words will announce itself by the "irruption of a new noise. . . .
Nothing heavy, nothing noisy; at most a murmur which will not add
anything to the great tumult of the cities which we think we suffer
under today. Its only character will be: it never stops. It is speaking,
it is as if the emptiness spoke, without mystery. The silence speaks."
There will be no refuge for a minority in libraries and museums. They
will be burned as Marinetti exhorted the Italians in 1909 to do, in
his desire to rid them of their burdensome past. In Blanchot's vision,
the dictator—from *dictare,* to say—will take the place of the writer,
the artist and the thinker. A deep despair about the future of mankind and of civilization speaks loudly through him and many others.
"The human voice conspires to desecrate everything on earth," says
J. D. Salinger. Still, if we reflect upon this indictment of literature
and language, we should recognize that it is man's actions, man's
tools and inventions, his whole society that are condemned here. Ad-
mittedly, civilization would be impossible or even completely different if man had not developed speech and writing, which have speeded
communication and prolonged human memory. But to deplore this,
as our apocalyptic prophets of doom and silence do so eloquently,
means deploring that man is man and not a dumb animal—a mood,
a gesture of despair but hardly a possible way of life and behavior.
Men will continue speaking, and even writing.

Less apocalyptically, literature and writing have been seen as a
transitory form of human communication to be replaced by the
media of the electronic age. We all know of Marshall McLuhan's
prophecy of the end of the Gutenberg era, his hope that our visual
literature will be replaced by the double medium, television, which he
argues is both aural and tactile. I won't enter into the difficulties of
his theories: they have been aired by critics who believe that television is just as visual as the film, despite his argument in *Understanding Media* that in television "the plastic contours appear by

light *through,* and not light *on,* and the image so formed has the quality of sculpture or icon rather than picture." McLuhan willfully confuses visibility and legibility. He cannot prove that literacy has impoverished the spoken language. There is, however, little doubt that the new media have made inroads into the reading habits particularly of youngsters, but for the present, there are no indications of any extinction of literacy, reading or the production of books. Any examination of statistics shows that book production and book sales have risen by leaps and bounds in all countries. In 1966, 460,000 new books were published. Even the usual assumption that the proportion of nonfiction compared to fiction has altered radically is not borne out by statistics. In Germany, as a recent article by Dieter Zimmer showed, fiction accounted for 16.4 percent of all book production in 1913 and for 19.5 percent in 1969. Nor is it true that book production is mainly reprinting of older literature. Of the 36,000 books published in West Germany alone in 1971, 85 percent were new books. Similar studies made for the United States, England and France yield similar results. The enormous expansion of the reading public in Eastern Europe and in the so-called Third World is an undeniable fact which makes the end of the Gutenberg era an event of the very far distant future.

All these attacks on literature, the politically motivated attack, the despair about the language, the retreat from the word, the cult of silence, and McLuhan's doubts about the future of literacy, assume a concept of literature that includes all acts of writing, from the most trivial to the most sublime. They make no distinction of quality, no aesthetic judgment.

The aesthetic concept of literature, the very concept of literature as art, has been under attack most insistently in recent decades. The collapse of aesthetics is the presupposition of the success of these attacks. The largely German theory of empathy, which reduces aesthetic feeling to the physical action of inner mimicry; the aesthetics of Benedetto Croce in which "intuition" is identified with any act of perception of individual quality—even of *this* glass of water; John Dewey's *Art as Experience* (1934), which denies all distinction between aesthetic and other experiences in favor of a unified, heightened vitality; I. A. Richards's writings on literary criticism, which abolish all distinction between aesthetic and other emotions, are just a few examples of this trend. More recently the analytical philosophers have tried to demonstrate "the dreariness of aesthetics," the "nonsense" of all traditional terms of aesthetics: beauty, form, and so on. Some of these criticisms are directed against aestheticism, the art for art's sake movement at the end of the last century, which set up art in an ivory tower or, contradictorily, claimed to make all life "beautiful." Chiding aestheticism as it deserved, the reaction against it involved its presumed ancestors: the founders of aesthetics, Kant, Schiller, Schelling and Hegel, none of whom would have ever dreamt of denying the enormous social and civilizing role of art. They were even extravagantly confident of its power. The aesthetic education propounded by Schiller was a scheme for freeing man from the necessities of nature and the evils of specialization.

The revolt against aesthetics was also a revolt against classical art with its demands for beauty, order, form, harmony and clarity of meaning. But such a desire to make things new was not a denial of the ideal of art or literature; rather it was an attempt at a redefinition of art or an extension of its meaning to allow for the innovations of the twentieth century. A German volume of conference papers and debates called *Die nicht mehr schönen Künste*, "the no longer fine arts" wittily formulates what has happened in recent decades: the inclusion in art of the ugly, the formless, the disorderly, the outrageous and obscene that culminated in Dada's thumbing its nose at art and echoes today in such movements as pop art. Attempts have been made not only to widen the realm of art but to abolish the boundary between art and nonart. In music, noises of machines or the streets are used; in painting, collages of stuck-on newspapers, or "found objects"—soup cans, bicycle wheels, electric bulbs, any piece of junk—are exhibited. The newest fad is "earthworks," holes or trenches in the ground, tracks through a cornfield, square sheets of lead in the snow. A "sculptor," Christo, wrapped a million square feet of Australian coastline in plastic. In poetry, poems have been concocted by Dadaists by drawing newspaper clippings from a bag at random; more recently poems have been produced by computer, and a shuffle novel (by Marc Saporta) has appeared, in which every page can be replaced by another in any order. In these new techniques the old criteria of both making and intentionality are denied: it is the extreme consequence of the rejection of the old conception of the poet as prophet, as *poeta-vates*, the laureate, the "unacknowledged legislator" with which the Western tradition has been familiar since Dante, Petrarch, Tasso, Milton and Shelley. The concept of inspiration is rejected: the new technological antiart divorces the poet from the poem, the artist from the object.

Yet another attack on literature leads to different consequences. It urges the same objection to defining literature by the quality of the art product. Northrop Frye's immensely influential and highly ingenious *Anatomy of Criticism* urges abolishing all critical judgment in favor of a concept of literature that makes it an organ of myth-making, a part of man's dream of self-definition. The result is that he can discuss any fairy tale, legend or detective story, as if it were on an equal footing with the greatest works of Dante, Shakespeare or Tolstoy. This breaking down of old barriers in favor of fictionality, myth-making, or "fabulation" must be distinguished from other attempts to disrupt the old concept. I am thinking of critics such as Leslie Fiedler and Richard Poirier, who want to extend the concept of literature to include what used to be called subliterature: pornography, science fiction and the popular song. Fiedler propagates a new, or possibly old, taste: in an essay, "The Children's Hour," the song full of "lovely commonplaces, long-honored phrases, sentimental clichés" is exalted; the tritest poems of Longfellow appear alongside poems of the Beatles, Bob Dylan and black antiverse, as Fiedler feels liberated, sincere for the first time. He can now repudiate Modernist poetry, "feel free at last to evoke in public the kind of poems which I have never ceased to love" but "which I've long felt obligated to recite in the catacombs, as it were." This assertion of a different taste, a return to the folksy, the sentimental, the direct expression of simple feelings, is the opposite of what is accomplished by computer poetry or by the graphic devices of so-called "concrete" poetry or even the automatic writings of surrealists. The dissolution of the concept of literature proceeds thus in two opposite directions: toward impersonal technology or toward subliterature.

Still, both these extensions of the concept of literature are within the realm of art. One can argue (as Louis Mink has, ingeniously) that even the most impersonal "found objects" can be salvage for art if we assume that the fact of their being singled out gives them some allegorical or iconographic meaning. Even the hospital urinal submitted by Marcel Duchamp or the grocery boxes of Andy Warhol are, somehow, works of art. They do express some rudimentary feeling. But the latest developments amount to a complete denial of art. Harold Rosenberg, in his new, aptly named book *The De-definition of Art,* quotes an artist as saying, "I choose not to make objects. Instead, I have set out to create a quality of experience which locates itself in the world." The artist has become too big for art: he regards anything he makes or does as art. "No one can say with assurance what a work of art is—or, more important, what is not a work of art." We can't distinguish between a masterpiece and junk. Nothing is left of art but the fiction of the artist. There is even more to be said for the extension of the concept of literature to oral literature, to mere yarn-spinning, or to the popular song that returns literature to its oral origins. French and English literature is largely bookish, but many literatures are still in close contact with their origins in oral folklore: in Eastern Europe, in Asia and in Africa. A meaningful concept of literature as a worldwide phenomenon reaching into the dim past of humanity will include what in English has been called, awkwardly enough, "oral literature." Father Ong complains that the term implies that "oral poetry should have been written down but somehow was not." Verbal art, *Wortkunst*, may be a better term: it would include Homer, whom Milman Parry has shown to belong to an oral tradition. But even much later, in the Middle Ages, the history of literature is incomprehensible without the constant interchange between the oral and the written word. Without sharing the taste for the sentimental banalities and comic obscenities admired by Leslie Fiedler, we should grant the fructification of modern literature by what the Russian formalists describe as the periodic need of "rebarbarization." We seem to be in such a period, and can only hope that it will achieve the results that at the end of the eighteenth century flowed from the rediscovery of Scottish ballads and Elizabethan songs in Percy's *Reliques of Ancient English Poetry*.

This incorporation of the popular arts, of oral literature in a total concept of literature cannot, however, ignore the aesthetic question: there is good and bad popular art, as there is good and bad upperclass art. Paul Elmer More, a lover of detective stories, graded his collection into categories A, B and C, and presumably the same could be done with science fiction or even pornography. The question of quality, the distinction between art and nonart, is unavoidable.

All these objections to the concepts of literature have one trait in common: they do not recognize quality as a criterion of literature: quality that may be either aesthetic or intellectual, but which in either case sets off a specific realm of verbal expression from daily transactions in language. This denial of quality runs counter to the whole long history of the term "literature" and the concept. It may be useful to glance at this history in order to see the debate in some perspective and to refute the strange notion of some recent commentators such as Maurice Blanchot and Roland Barthes, who consider the term and concept creations of the nineteenth century. What I can give is only a brief sketch for a topic that deserves a book-length study.

The term *literatura*, which obviously comes from *litera*, "letter" in Latin, was called by Quintilian a translation of the Greek *grammatiké*: it thus meant simply a knowledge of reading and writing. Cicero, however, speaks of Julius Caesar as having *literatura* in a list of his qualities that includes "good sense, memory, reflection and diligence." It must mean here something like "literary culture." We have to go to Tertullian and Cassian in the second century after

Christ to find the term used for a body of writing. They contrast secular *literatura* with *scriptura,* pagan with Christian literature.

Much more prevalent, however, was the term *litterae* in Rome. Cicero speaks of *Graecae litterae* and of *studium humanitatis ac litterarum.* Aulus Gellius expressly identifies *humanitas* with the Greek *paideia; litterae* in antiquity are simply the study of the arts and letters of the Greeks as far as they represent the Greek idea of man. In practice the study of letters was the study of the Greek writers, of Homer and the writers of the Periclean age. I need not enter into the remote history of the rise of this conception in opposition to the oral tradition crystallized in the Homeric poems. Eric Havelock's *Preface to Plato* traced this evolution persuasively.

In the Middle Ages the terms were used rarely. *Literatus* or *literator* meant anybody acquainted with the art of reading and writing. With the establishment of the seven liberal arts, including the trivium, literature as a term seems to have disappeared, although poetry was recognized as an art assigned to grammar and rhetoric.

With the Renaissance a clear consciousness of a new secular literature emerges and with it the terms *litterae humanae, lettres humaines, bonnes lettres,* or as late as Dryden, "good letters." These terms were used widely by Rabelais, Du Bellay, Montaigne and other French writers of the sixteenth century. In the seventeenth century the term "belles-lettres" emerged. In 1666 Charles Perrault proposed to Colbert, the minister of finance of Louis XIV, an Academy with a section of belles-lettres, which was to include grammar, eloquence and poetry. The term, as dictionaries show, was felt to be identical with *lettres humaines* and had nothing of the faintly derisive implication with which we today speak of the "belletristic." The French term spread quickly to England: Thomas Rymer used it in 1692. Hugh Blair became professor of rhetoric and belles-lettres at the University of Edinburgh in 1762.

By that time the term "literature" had reemerged in the sense of a knowledge of literature, of literary culture. La Bruyère speaks, in 1688, of "men of agreeable literature." Voltaire calls Chapelain a man of "immense literature" and in a dictionary article, defines literature as "a knowledge of the works of taste, a smattering of history, poetry, eloquence and criticism." Marmontel, Voltaire's follower, terms literature a "knowledge of belles-lettres" and contrasts it expressly with erudition. "With wit, talent, and taste," he promises, "one can produce ingenious works, without any erudition, and with little literature."

In English, the same meaning became established. Thus the antiquary John Selden was, in 1691, called "a person of infinite literature" and Boswell refers to Giuseppe Baretti as an "Italian of considerable literature." The use of the term survived in the nineteenth century when John Petherham wrote *A Sketch of the Progress and Present State of Anglo-Saxon Literature in England* (1840), where literature must mean the study of literature. (Incidentally, in the term "comparative literature," this older usage survives. It obviously means the comparative study of literatures and is not, as Lane Cooper complained, a "bogus term which makes neither sense nor syntax.")

Apparently, in the thirties of the eighteenth century the term "literature" began to be used as a designation for a body of writing. It occurs in François Granet's little-known *Réflexions sur les ouvrages de littérature* in 1737, and soon afterward in Voltaire. In Germany, Lessing applied it clearly to a body of writing in his *Briefe die neueste Literatur betreffend*. Tiraboschi's *Storia della letteratura italiana* is, I believe, the first work with the term on the title page. In England, the same shift of meaning took place. The New English Dictionary quotes the first example for "body of writing" in 1822. But George Coleman the elder thought in 1761 that "Shakespeare and Milton seem to stand alone, like first rate authors, amid the general wreck of old English literature." In 1778 Dr. Johnson wished, in a letter, that "what is undeservedly forgotten of our antiquated literature might be revived." Other examples from the later eighteenth century are not infrequent. Still, the first book in English called a *History of English Language and Literature,* by Robert Chambers, dates only from 1836.

In all the early uses literature and letters are used inclusively. The terms refer to many kinds of writing, not only the imaginative, but also writing of an erudite nature, to historiography, theology, philosophy and so on. Only much later was the term narrowed down to what we call today "imaginative literature," poetry and imaginative prose. The earliest clear declaration of this new use that I know of is in the preface to Carlo Denina's *Discorso sopra le vicende della letteratura* (1760), a book that was soon translated into French and English. Denina professes "not to speak of the progress of sciences and arts, which are not properly a part of literature." He will speak of works of learning only when they belong to "good taste, to eloquence, that is to say, to literature." That literature was used in this aesthetic sense at that time may be illustrated by the title of A. de Giorgo-Bertóla's *Idea della letteratura alemanna* (1784), which is an expanded version of an earlier *Idea della poesia alemanna* (1770); the change of title was forced by the inclusion of a new chapter on German novels, particularly on Goethe's *Sorrows of the Young Werther.*

To speak sweepingly, one can say that in older times, in antiquity and in the Renaissance, literature or letters was understood to include all writing of quality with any pretense to permanence. Poetry was set apart mainly because of the clear distinction made by verse. The view that there is an art of literature, a verbal art that includes poetry and prose as far as it is imaginative fiction, and thus excludes information and even rhetorical persuasion or didactic argumentation, emerged slowly with the whole system of the modern arts. It took about a century to prepare for Kant's *Critique of Judgment* (1790), which gave a clear formulation for distinguishing the good, the true and the useful from the beautiful. The slow rise in the prestige of the novel, long frowned upon as frivolous, collaborated in establishing a concept of literature parallel to the plastic arts and to music.

The meaning of a word is that given to it by its users. We cannot prevent anybody from speaking about campaign literature or about the literature relating to a pharmaceutical product. "Literature" has been and can be used to refer to anything in print. On the other hand it has more often meant, as I have shown, literary culture, the whole tradition of humane letters descending from antiquity. It meant for centuries works valued for their intellectual or imaginative eminence. In the eighteenth century the term often was narrowed down to cover all imaginative literature: the novel, the epic, the lyric poem, the play. In English the word "poetry" is limited more narrowly to works in verse. We cannot speak, as the Germans do, of Dostoevsky or Kafka as a *Dichter*. It is the way I have used the term "literature" in *Theory of Literature*. Often, of course, literature has been contrasted with poetry. Thus Benedetto Croce made a distinction between *letteratura* and *poesia*. *Letteratura* has a great civilizing function, but *poesia* stands apart, outside of history, limited to the great peaks of what we would call imaginative literature. Sartre in *What Is Literature?* draws the same distinction but values it differently. Literature is writing committed to changing man's consciousness, while poetry is assigned only a little nook and corner safely hidden from the stresses of history and historical change. Literature also has been used as a pejorative term for empty rhetoric, as in Verlaine's well-known poem *Art poétique*. He wanted to "wring the neck of eloquence"; he exalted music in poetry and concluded "Et tout le reste est littérature."

In understanding these lexical distinctions we shall be able to reject the wholesale attack on literature: the political attack, which makes literature a reactionary force although it obviously can be and has been the opposite; the linguistic attack, which despairs of the very possibility of speech; and the antiaesthetic attack, which revolts against quality and form in favor of subliterature or the impersonal permutations of the computer. Finally, the replacement of literature by the new media will seem a very unlikely event of the distant future. None of these theories touches the capacity of man to create works of literature also in the future. The forms of literature will no doubt change radically, but as long as there is man in any conceivable shape he will create—that is, speak, express and communicate in writing and in print his observations, his feelings, his desires, his ideas and his probings into himself and the nature of the world around him. Doubts about the exact limits of literature cannot obviate the difference between art and nonart, great and bad art, a Shakespeare play and a newspaper poem, a story by Tolstoy and a story in *True Confessions*. Doubts about language and its reach can only sharpen the poet's struggle to achieve what is difficult to formulate in language and to make him and us suspicious of the debasement of the word in propaganda, advertising and bad journalism. Predictions of the end of literacy, of the triumph of television, should make us more aware of the need of a literary culture. The new barbarism, the know-nothingism, the mindless repudiation of the past in favor of so-called "relevance"— one trusts that these are only a passing mood of this country and decade of ours. We may reflect that this crisis of the concept of literature is confined to small, largely academic circles in France and the United States. It also flourishes among a group of neo-Marxists in Western Germany. It has not, I think, affected England, although in the writings of Raymond Williams and Richard Hoggart the uses of culture and literacy have been subjected to a stringent examination. Doubts about literature and its uses are, I think, completely absent in the Communist world because there literature has been made a tool for the education and indoctrination of the masses.

We cannot predict the shape of things to come: in 1872 nobody could have forecast, in any detail, the literary situation as it is today. But there remain basic certainties: there will be, I am sure, no silence, no incessant murmur, as forecast by Blanchot. There will still be the voices of men of letters and poets, in verse or prose, who will speak (as they have done since hoary antiquity) for their society and for mankind. Mankind will always need a voice and a record of that voice in writing and print, in literature.

PART THREE

the future: literacy and the media

The doubts about literacy expressed in previous chapters have been paralleled by increased concern for the content and techniques of oral communication in nonliterate societies, and for the remnants of oral culture that have survived within literate civilizations. Many writers, such as the novelist Mulk Raj Anand, fear that the growth of literacy in semiliterate India will harm that part of the cultural heritage which is still based on the oral tradition:

> Although the printed word was not available [in India] until a hundred years ago, there was no lack of knowledge in . . . oral culture. Over the previous three thousand years of known history . . . some of the wisest men in the world flourished there, from the philosophers of the *Upanishads,* to prophets like the Buddha, the medieval saints, mystics, bards and poets. The vast population of illiterates . . . had a mnemonic tradition of the proverb and the moral story, of myth and legend, which shows evidence of the highest culture. The age of print may . . . have led to more external progress, but it may have also frightened off the shy birds of sensibility . . . which are India's precious cultural heritage.

Nevertheless, even among those like Anand who value most highly the "shy birds of sensibility" that can survive only within an oral tradition, few believe that universal literacy should not remain one of humanity's major goals.

Yet as the developing nations move toward full literacy the West may be simultaneously developing a form of aural-oral culture of its own. Our reluctance to admit this is, according to Walter Ong, S.J., a consequence of the powerful psychological hold that typographic literacy has on the Western mind. He argues that people in literate culture "structure their entire world around a feel for the written word to the positive (but not often conscious) exclusion of the oral as such." Now, however, there are indications that we are overcoming this reluctance, and that the role of orality in literate societies is slowly gaining both recognition and prestige.

One important influence is the emphasis in modern linguistics research on the primacy of oral over written sources for understanding how language works. This development is important because literacy and literary culture have for centuries been tied to social mobility, class consciousness, and cultural elitism. With print came the grammar book, "proper" speech, and linguistic snobbery. Now many experts accept all languages and their dialects as equally valid methods of communication. There is no longer a reasonable definition of "superior" speech or "pure" English. There are, instead, many different ways to communicate through words. Some work better for one purpose, some for another.

The present acrimonious debate over the teaching of "black English" and other so-called dialects is another indication that oral communication is gaining recognition as a valuable medium for transmitting cultural information. The debate is unavoidably involved with the familiar shibboleths about literacy, including the link between literacy and economic advancement. Those who favor teaching Standard English to blacks (instead of allowing black children to use their own idiomatic speech) argue that conformity to white English, patterned on the *Reader's Digest, The Atlantic,* and the speech of television broadcasters, is a prerequisite to making it in the "real" world. Their opponents argue that children suffer psychological damage when, forced to master a strange idiom, they suspect (or are told) that their inherited idiom is inferior, and that the teaching of Standard English is a subtle form of cultural genocide.

Whatever the merits on either side, the concern for the form and content of spoken language reveals that a new credence is being given to the ways people actually speak, rather than to the ways some people think they should speak.

Thus there are important signs that print culture is undergoing a genuine revaluation, and that the function of print in Western society is likely to be seriously modified as a consequence. On the other hand, as Ben Bagdikian points out in "Is Print Dying?," there are many reasons to believe that alphabetic communication will continue to have important functions within electronic media systems. Undoubtedly much new technology, such as microprinting, laser writing, holography, and computer printouts will help print survive. And, according to most estimates by UNESCO and other organizations, illiteracy rates are likely to decrease rapidly in the next two decades creating new demand for books and periodicals.

Unquestionably there are many functional uses for print that will enable it to survive into the foreseeable future. But a more important test will certainly involve its aesthetic uses and its capacity to sustain the literary impulse that gave birth to the novel, the essay, journalism, and other forms of typographic art—the "full literacy" that George Steiner discusses in "After the Book?"

In Steiner's opinion the absolute conditions required to sustain the high literacy of the past have been so seriously undermined by a variety of environmental changes that we have already entered the "postcultural" situation. While the functional uses of print will likely survive, the outlook for the spiritual-aesthetic uses and for literary culture in general is increasingly dim.

A somewhat different point of view is expressed by Edmund Carpenter in his essay "Not Since Babel." Carpenter believes that young dropouts are creating an underground readership for the classics, which they are "removing" from the deadening influences of most literary criticism and scholarly nit-picking. Certainly the past twenty years have seen youth bring Herman Hesse, Kurt Vonnegut, and Richard Brautigan to the campus. Now, Carpenter believes, the fleeing dropouts are carrying away the very classics they refused to read for their professors.

Obviously, then, there are major disagreements among media experts that make prediction a hazardous indulgence. Whatever the case, the future of literacy will, ultimately, be determined by the dialectical process between print culture and the future, between the cognitive, analytical "mind" of literate man and the non-cognitive perceptions of the electronic sensibility, tied as it is to total involvement in sound and image.

Chapter 13

after the book?*

George Steiner

It is like us to ask such questions. They are, in several ways, symptomatic of the present climate of feeling. We are ready to ask very large and inherently destructive questions. This is radicalism in a special sense. Not Hegelian-Marxist radicalism with its implicit futurity, with its almost axiomatic presumption that we go to the root of a problem in order to solve it, and because we know that destruction, uprooting is only a necessary risk before solution. No; our going to the root of things is more ambivalent. We would do so even when we are not confident that there *is* a solution. It may be, in fact, that the aspect of demolition, the apocalyptic strain greatly tempt us. We are fascinated by "last things," by the end of cultures, of ideologies, of art forms, of modes of sensibility. We are, certainly since Nietzsche and Spengler, "terminalists." Our view of history, says Lévi-Strauss in a deep pun, is not an anthropology but an "entropology."

This makes for intellectual exhilaration and a kind of bleak nobility. It is, presumably, not every species that can meditate its own ruin, not every society that can image its own decay and possible subjection to new and alien energies. But it is a negative radicalism which carries with it an element of self-fulfilment. This is a large, intricate topic. As I have tried to show elsewhere, a good deal of the barbarism of the politics of our century was anticipated, dreamt of, fantasized about in the art, literature, and apocalyptic theories of the previous

* [Originally given as an address to the Ferguson Seminar in Publishing at The College of William and Mary, March 23, 1972.—Ed.]

hundred years. It makes sense—although only in a dialectical way—to ask whether a force of prevision of the order of Kafka's does not in some manner "prepare," "prepare for" the lunacies and inhumanities which it intimates. If we ask, therefore, whether there is a future for books or what may come after the end of books, we may be doing more than pose a question. The fact that we *can* and *do* ask may be part of the process of debilitation which, presumably, we fear; and it could, conceivably, hasten it. It is a famous saying of Marx that mankind does not ask major questions until there is the objective possibility of an answer. This may be so. But there is another, more disturbing way of putting it: mankind may only ask certain questions in order to elicit a negative, predictive reply.

Obviously, however, we are not meeting in a spirit of indifferent inquiry or nihilistic play. If we pose the question of the viability of the book, it is because we find ourselves in a social, psychological, technical situation which gives this question substance. And although we hope to press the question home and to look scrupulously at the evidence, we hope also that the question will resolve itself positively; that our asking is, in Hegel's incisive terminology, an *Aufhebung*. Asking is an action, a possible bringing into view and into being of perspectives in which the question is seen to be trivial or falsely posed. Or, at the rare best, to ask is to provoke not the answer one actually fears or aims at, but the first contours of a new and better asking—which is then a first kind of answer. Bearing this in mind, let us sketch very briefly some of the historical and pragmatic grounds which make it possible and even responsible to envisage the end of the book as we have known it.

First, it is worth stressing that the "book as we have known it" has been a significant phenomenon only in certain areas and cultures, and only during a relatively short span of history. Being bookmen we tend to forget the extremely special locale and circumstances of our addiction. We lack anything like a comprehensive history of reading. It would, I think, show that reading in our sense—"with unmoving lips" —does not predate St. Augustine (who first remarked on it) by very much. But I would narrow the range even further. The existence of the book as a common, central fact of personal life depends on economic, material, educational preconditions which hardly predate the late sixteenth century in western Europe and in those regions of the earth under direct European influence. Montaigne and Bacon are already bookmen, and profoundly conscious of the relations of their own inner life to the future of the printed form. But even they read in a way which is not entirely ours; their sense of the authority, of the layered hermeticism of the written word—from surface level to anagogical mystery—has much in common with an earlier, almost pictorial or "iconic" view of meaning. Our style of reading, the unforced currency of our business with books, is not easy to document before, say, Montesquieu. It climaxes in Mallarmé's well-known pronouncement that the true aim of the universe, of all vital impulse, is the creation of a supreme book—*le Livre*. Now the relevant time span is only about a century and a half. Yet it is undoubtedly true that Mallarmé himself marks the beginning of the questions we are asking here.

The classic age of the book depended on a number of material factors (even as we have no full history of reading, we have no sociology of reading, though there are in the criticism of Walter Benjamin and in Adorno's sociology of music numerous indications as to what is needed).

The book on the monastery lectern or in the chained university library is not the same as that of the seventeenth century. In its classic phase, the book is a privately owned object. This requires the conjunction of specific possibilities of production, marketing, and storage. The private library is far more than an architectural device. It concentrates a very complicated spectrum of social and psychological values. It requires and, in turn, determines certain allocations of space and silence which impinge on the house as a whole. In visual and tactile terms, it favours particular formats or genres—the two are intimately meshed—over others: say the bound volume over the pamphlet, the in-octavo over the folio, the *opera omnia* or set over the single title. The spiritual cannot be divorced from the physical fact. A man sitting alone in his personal library reading is at once the product and begetter of a particular social and moral order. It is a *bourgeois* order founded on certain hierarchies of literacy, of purchasing power, of leisure, and caste. Elsewhere in the house there is most likely a domestic who dusts the shelves of books, who enters the library when called. And there are children schooled not to make undue noise, not to burst in when their father is reading. In short, the classic act of reading—what is depicted as *la lecture* in so many eighteenth-century genre paintings and engravings—is the focus of a number of implicit power relations between the educated and the menial, between the leisured and the exhausted, between space and crowding, between silence and noise, between the sexes and the generations (it is only very gradually that women come to read in the same way and context as their husbands, brothers, and fathers).

These power relations and value-assumptions have been drastically eroded. There are few libraries now in private apartments and fewer servants to dust them or oil the book spines. Intensities of light and noise levels of an unprecedented volume crowd in on personal space, particularly in the urban home. Far more often than not, the act of reading takes place against, in direct competition with another medium—television, radio, the record player. There are almost no taboo-spaces or sacrosanct hours left in the modern family. All is free zone. Where the book shelves were, we tend to find the record cabinet and the row of l-p's (this, in itself, is one of the most important changes in the climate, in the enveloping matrix of our intellectual and emotional lives). It is only rarely in the home that the exercise of reading, in the old sense, now takes place. It is in highly specialized frameworks: mainly the university library or academic "office." We are almost back at the stage before Montaigne's famous circular reading room in the quiet tower. We read "seriously" as did the clerics, in special professional places, where books are professional tools and silence is institutional.

The modern paperback is an immediate and brilliantly efficient embodiment of the new parameters. It takes very little space. It is quasi-disposable. Its compactness declares that it can be, is almost intended to be, used "in motion," under casual and fragmented circumstances. Being quite explicitly of the same material make-up as trashfiction, the paperback—even where its content is high-brow— proclaims an easy democracy of access. It carries with it no manifest sign of economic or cultural élitism. Mickey Spillane and Plato share the same book rack in the airport lounge or drug store. But the mainsprings of change in the status of the book lie deeper. Definite philosophic beliefs and habits of perception underlay the primacy of the book in the life of the mind from the time of Descartes to that of Thomas Mann (one of the last complete representatives of the classic stance). Having tried to make some of these points in detail in previous work, I will do no more than summarize.

In very large measure, most books are about previous books. This is true at the level of the semantic code: writing persistently refers to previous writing. Explicit or implicit citation, allusion, reference are essential means of designation and proposition. It is via this dynamism of reiteration that the past has its most palpable existence. But the process of reference is even more comprehensive. Grammar, the literary idiom, a genre such as a sonnet or a prose novel, embody a previous formalization of numan experience. Thoughts, feelings, events as set down in books do not come raw; the format of expression carries with it very strong and complex, though often "subliminal," values and boundaries. In a suggestive essay, some years ago, E. H. Gombrich showed that even the most violent, spontaneous of pictorial notations —Goya's sketches of the insurrection in Madrid—are stylized by, filtered through previous works of art. So it is with books: all literature has behind it human experience of the kind which previous literature has identified as meaningful. The act of writing for the printed page as it conjoins with the reading response is intensely "axiomatized" or conventionalized, however fresh and turbulent the author's impulse. The past is strongly at his back; the current moves between bounds of established possibility.

These elements of tradition and limitation are of the essence of a classic world view. If western literature—from Homer and Ovid to *Ulysses* and *Sweeny Among the Nightingales*—has been so largely referential, each major work mirroring what has gone before and bending the light only so much out of a given focus and no more, the reason lies at the very heart of our literacy. Western and Chinese culture have been bookish in a very definite way: Western culture unfolds, by highly self-conscious modes of imitation, variation, renascence, parody, or *pastiche*, from a strikingly small set of canonic, classical texts and form-models, principally Greek. By creative "ingestion," as Ben Jonson put it, the curve of discourse tends from Homer to Virgil, from Virgil to Dante, from Dante to Milton, Klopstock, Joyce, and the explicit retrospective of the *Cantos*. There have been fifteen *Oresteias* and a dozen *Antigones* in twentieth-century drama and opera. Archilocus points to Horace, Horace to Jonson, Jonson to Dryden and Landor, Landor to Robert Graves. The line, the experience of lament over the poet or hero who has died young is unbroken since the Greek Anthology and passes, via stages of massive cross-reference, through *Lycidas* and *Adonais* to Arnold's *Thyrsis,* Tennyson's *In Memoriam,* and Auden's elegy—built of Ovidian echoes—on the passing of Yeats. Print and the physique of books have been the enforcing framework of tradition. It is in this respect—not in any vague, undemonstrable intimation of visual-linear compulsion—that we can characterize western culture as being that of the library at Alexandria, of Gutenberg and of Caxton.

This close correlation of formal invention, of energized feeling with established genres and a framework of allusion and prepared echo has further implications. *Le Livre* is the proven talisman against death. This is the grand discovery, the proud cry, in Homer and Pindar: the words of the poet outlive the events they narrate and make the poet immortal. Rephrased by Horace and by Ovid the promise that time cannot gnaw great words to dust, that they will outlast the brass and marble on which they are incised, is the password of western literature. I die, my life may have been a shamble of error and non-recognition, but if my book has truth and beauty enough, it will endure. There are those as yet unborn who shall read it, as I read the classic on my table. This is the secret of Demodocus, the minstrel in the *Odyssey,* and, two and a half millennia later, of Paul Éluard when he states *le dur désir de durer.*

The gamble on immortality can only come off if language itself holds. There is nothing mystical about this notion. It is a traditional trope of western literature, particularly poetry, that words are inadequate to the needs of personal expression, that available language falls drastically short of the poet's inner vision. But this trope is itself linguistically articulated. The anguish of unattainable precision or radiance is real enough, but it is also conventional and is itself a means of eloquence. The Petrarchian sonnet springs constantly and with confident elaboration from a basic complaint about its own insufficiency to state the uniqueness, the vehemence of the poet's love. Mystical writings, such as the *Canciones* of St. John of the Cross come nearest the limit; but we know this just because they communicate to us in words of great precision and clarity their sense of the neighbourhood of the inexpressible.

Here again, the complex of the book and of its reader stands in a specific Judaic-Hellenic descent. It is from these two antique sources, so oddly, so intensely literary and bookish in their self-definition, that we derive our view of the eminent worth and stability of speech. These two civilizations tell us that the word—the *logos*—is central to man's religion, to his *log*ic, to his mytho*log*ies. They tell us that the relations of descriptive adequacy between human language and the "outside world" may be epistemologically opaque, that there are deep problems about meaning what we say and saying what we mean, about understanding one another and about denoting objects or sense-data unambiguously. Nonetheless, this very opaqueness can only be diagnosed and registered in words, linguistically. We inhabit a language-world, and if it is the source of perplexing but marginal dilemmas, it is also the root of our conscious being and mastery over nature.

This conviction, of which books are the active incarnation, prevails with only eccentric challenges from the time of the great oral epics at least to that of Rimbaud and Surrealism.

Each of these philosophic tenets and the psychological attitudes which accompany them have come under severe attack. (Perhaps one ought to have realized earlier how fragile the fabric of western literacy was, how delicate and probably unique were the historical, moral raw materials which went into its making.)

The basis of referential recognition on which our poetry and prose have operated from Chaucer to T. S. Eliot, from the *Roman de la rose* to Valéry, has become the increasingly fictive possession of a mandarin few. The organized amnesia of American schooling—and much of Europe is following suit—ensures that the alphabet of scriptural, mythological, historical allusion in our literature has become a hieroglyphic. Footnotes lengthen on the page as rudimentary identifications and paraphrase are needed. Off balance on top of these explanatory stilts, the poem itself becomes strange and blurred. More and more of our verbal inheritance is caught between the semi-literacy of the mass market and the Byzantine minutiae of the specialist. In the glass case of the academic storehouse verse, drama, fiction which was once a common presence now leads an immaculate but factitious life. Authority—and authority is the core, the wellspring of formal tradition—is itself highly suspect. Ezra Pound's "make it new" was, in fact, a call for renovation in the renaissance sense. The cry of the new millenarians against the classic, against eloquence, against that which is difficult of access, is something entirely different. It goes back to the terrorist insight of Dada that the literate past must be destroyed, dynamited if history is to enter a phase of radical innocence.

The aim of survival, of glory in the pantheon, is equally suspect. It speaks of hierarchy and academicism. We seem to be involved in a revolution of time-values. *Now* is everything, and the young regard as hypocrisy, opportunism, or worse, the traditional strategy of the poet or thinker sacrificing his present life to future eminence. This equivocation, self-evident to Milton, to Keats, to Hölderlin, now has a ring of hallow bathos. To the radical generation there is obscenity in Mallarmé's belief that a supreme masterpiece, *le Livre,* is the goal and validation of human affairs. Today Pisarev's slogan, "a pair of boots outweighs Shakespeare and Pushkin," has come into its own.

The doubts about language have more varied and respectable sources. Again, I have dealt with this theme at length previously and will only summarize here. In the period from Rimbaud and Mallarmé to Dada and Surrealism an "anti-language" movement springs up from inside literature. Bored by the oppressive eloquence and perfections of the past, the new iconoclasts and experimenters sought to recreate the word, to find in new verbal and syntactic forms intact resources of exactitude, of magic, of sub-conscious energy. The Dada demand for "an end to the word" is at once nihilistic—man cannot be renewed if he keeps his worn skin of speech—and aesthetic. It calls for the discovery of hitherto unexploited phonetic, iconic, and semiological means. A second current of doubt is that which stems from formal logic and the work of logical positivism and of Wittgenstein. It is one of the major effects of modern philosophy, from Moore to Austin and

Quine, to have made language look messier, more fragile, less comfortably concordant with our needs, than before. The confidence in the medium which animates earlier philosophic monuments—those of Kant, of Hegel, of Schopenhauer, of Bergson—is simply no longer available. A third impulse to linguistic scepticism comes from the enormous expansion of the exact sciences. An ever-increasing portion of sensory and conceptual reality has passed into the keeping of the non-verbal semantic systems of mathematics. A modern writer can deal precisely, and in the relevant idiom, with far less of natural fact and intellectual analysis than could Shakespeare, Milton, or Pope. The fourth aspect is that first investigated by Karl Kraus and George Orwell: the cheapening, the dehumanization, the muddling of words through the mass media and through the lies of barbarism of modern politics. This brutalization and profanation of the word is very probably one of the main causes for the tide of self-destruction, either through self-imposed silence or actual suicide, which has come over western literature from the time of Nerval and Rimbaud to that of Sylvia Plath, Paul Celan, and John Berryman. The words in my mouth, says Ionesco, have gone dead.

Taken together, these attacks on traditional literacy, on the transcendental view of the artist's and thinker's enterprise, and on the validity of language constitute a fundamental critique of the book. It is not so much a "counter-culture" which is being developed, but a "post-culture."

But once we have made this analysis, the factual question arises: *are* people reading less, is there an empirically demonstrable decline in the vitality of printed books?

The evidence is very difficult to come by. Robert Escarpit's *La Révolution du livre* (1966) is the only full-scale study I know of, and it is at best, preliminary. What we find are fragments of information, isolated statistics, guesses of every kind. I hesitate even to adduce these in the presence of experts.

A survey conducted in 1970 indicates that on average a French man or woman will read no more than *one* book a year. The figure for Italy is thought to be even less as there are extensive pockets of sub-literacy. In Germany, on the other hand, the ratio is rather better. The number of bookstores in the United States—i.e., of stores primarily or exclusively devoted to the sale of serious books and able to keep a representative selection in stock—has diminished drastically over the past twenty years (I have heard the figure of closures of "hybridizations" put as high as 75%). The turn-over rate has accelerated formidably, especially in regard to fiction. If it is not immediately successful, a new novel will remain only very briefly in the bookstore. The ratio of remaindered prose fiction to what is kept in stock from among the estimated thirty or forty novels published weekly in the English language is, obviously, dramatic. The economics of serious hard-cover publishing have become fairly lunatic. Prices have trebled and often quadrupled between successive volumes in the same work or series. In numerous cases publication would not be feasible at all were it not for complex, often hidden schemes of subsidization or for immediate tie-ups with the paperback market. It is, currently, no more than a sober platitude that the whole future of the commercial production and distribution of hard-cover books with only a limited circulation is in doubt. The wild circus of personnel changes among American publishing houses, the spate of take-overs, the febrile vulgarization of once-great lists, are only the external symptom of a deep malaise in the whole book-world.

To these facts I would add one or two personal observations, obviously subjective and very limited in scope. Paperbacks do *not* make for the collection of a library. Among the very many students I have met and taught in several countries over the past two decades, fewer and fewer are book collectors, fewer and fewer reject the pre-packaged selectivity of the paperback in order to own *complete* works of an author. Among these same young people there appears to be a marked decline in habits of solitary, exclusive reading. They know less and less of literature *by heart*. They read against a musical background or in company. Almost instinctively, they resent the solipsism, the egotistical claims on space and silence implicit in the classic act of reading. They wish to shut no one out from the empathic tide of their consciousness. Being something we can listen to personally yet share fully with others at the same moment and in the same place, music, far more than books, meets the present ideal of participatory response. It is not the "dog-eared volume" we find in the walker's pocket, but the transistor. And because it allows access at so many levels—ranging from technical insight to the vague wash of semi-conscious echo— music allows that democracy of emotion which literature, particularly difficult literature, denies. In brief: so far as I can make out, the prime requisites of concentrated reading in the old sense—aloneness, silence, contextual recognitions—are growing rare in the very milieu in which we would most crucially look for them—that of the undergraduate.

These are, I repeat, *ad hoc* and piecemeal impressions. They are nearly impossible to quantify. We are too close to these new tendencies and problems to have more than a very indistinct view. My observations would, I suspect, not be true of the Soviet Union, which is in a phase of centrally determined, almost Victorian literacy. They are only partly true of those countries of eastern Europe in which reading is often the best way of showing opposition to the regime, and in which competing electronic media remain underdeveloped. Nevertheless, and with regard to our own setting, I would say that the world of the bookman is much diminished.

Hence one's readiness to speculate—it can be no more than that—on what may come after the book or what may happen to books in a period of cultural transition.

It is now a commonplace that audio-visual means of communication are taking over wide areas of information, persuasion, entertainment which were, formerly, the domain of print. At a time of global increase in semi- or rudimentary literacy (true literacy is, as I have tried to suggest, in fact decreasing), it is very probable that audio-visual "culture packages," i.e. in the guise of casettes, will play a crucial role. It is already, I think, fair to say that a major portion of print, as it is emitted daily, is, at least in the broad sense of the term, a caption. It accompanies, it surrounds, it draws attention to material which is essentially pictorial. When uttered on the radio and, to a far greater degree, when spoken on television, language has a specialized, perhaps ancillary status. The phenomenon can be exaggerated: contrary to McLuhan's expectations, radio is holding its own, particularly in such hyper-verbal genres as discussion or drama. It is nonetheless obvious that a great part of humanity now receives its main informational and evocative stimuli in the form of images and illustrative signal-codes. The astonishing fact is not that this should be so, but that the word in the old sense should still be so vital. We touch here on an extremely puzzling phenomenon. Even the most superb of movies can only be seen a very limited number of times (say five or six) before it goes stale, before an impression of utter inertness takes over. Why should this be? In what way is a piece of print—a poem, a chapter in a novel, a scene from a play—any less "fixed," static, unchanging than a film frame? Yet we can read the same poem a hundred times over in our lives and it will literally be new to us. Where does the difference lie? What is there about purely visual material which does not have the inherent repeatability, the sameness with change which is the attribute of the written word? So far as I know, neither aesthetics nor psychology have come up with an answer. But the evidence is, I believe, unmistakable, and it entails a power of survival for printed speech which no competing medium has.

The more radical, though less visible changes, are those occurring not in the communication of material but in its storage and analytic treatment. Information storage and retrieval by means of data banks and computers are far more than technical devices. They constitute little less than a new way of organizing human knowledge and the relations of present inquiry to past work. All taxonomies are, in essense, philosophical. Any library system, whether by size or Dewey, enacts a formalized vision of how the world is put together, of what are the optimal sight-lines between the human mind and phenomenological totality. Electronic indexing and memorization, the instant provision of information according to various grids and semantic markers, will profoundly alter not only the physical structure of libraries, but our proceedings in them. The key concepts of referential relevance and of context (the books further down the shelf, the one we needed most but did not know we were looking for) will change. Data banks are not for browsing. In many disciplines, moreover, the cutoff point of chronological utility will be codified and institutionalized. One will not be expected to cite, to be aware of material earlier than a very recent point on the index tape. It will thus become ever more difficult to resist the illusion—and it *is* an illusion, certainly so far as most humanities go—that insight is cumulative, that there is a necessary progress and teleology in the statement of feelings and ideas. The "programming" of knowledge in the electronically managed libraries of the future will, I think, bring on alterations of sensibility, modifications in our habits of discovery, as significant as any since the invention of moveable type. The formula is one that makes for the minimalization of hazard, of waste, of spill-over. Yet it is these counter-utilitarian aspects of traditional reading which have determined much of the best in our culture.

What of the more immediate prospects for the printed book? In the presence of some of those most competent in the field, it is perhaps foolhardy to conjecture. But some lines of change are already clear. There will be fewer books published. The current rate of overproduction, notably in fiction, has triggered an absurd, ultimately self-defeating spiral of small printings, mounting overheads and the inability to amortize costs at anything near the rate regarded as indispensable in other industries. There will be fewer publishers, and it looks as if the edition and production of books, in both England and America, is passing into the hands of a small number of large consortia, often allied with, financed by other industries or capital holdings. What seems to be emerging is a pattern of giants together with a few small, specialized houses whose actual structure resembles that of the "little magazine" in relation to the mass media. The search for a technological breakthrough in regard to production costs will intensify. The restrictive and inflationary practices in the printing trades plainly reflect a luddite, terminal mood. The industry feels that its days are numbered. Whether some radical new photoprocess will emerge, whether the electric typewriter points the way, is uncertain. But increasingly, the hard-cover book printed (let alone illustrated) by traditional manual-mechanical means, is an anachronism. It is viable only in very large editions, which are of course limited to a small percentage of the annual list.

Even more significantly, there will, I expect, be a frank polarization in our understanding of books and of what is meant by *reading*. A firmer distinction than has been current hitherto will emerge as between the immense iceberg bulk of semi-attentive reading—ranging from the advertisement billboard to the pulp novel—and genuine "full" reading. The latter will, more and more, become the craft and pursuit of a minority trained to do the job and who themselves probably hope to write a book. It is precisely the disaster of mass education in the United States, but also in other over-developed consumer technocracies, to have blurred this vital difference. A large majority of those who passed through the primary and secondary school system can "read" but not *read*. Theirs is a pseudo-literacy. Various measurements are possible. It has been estimated that the vocabulary and grammatical comprehension possessed by a considerable majority of American adults has stabilized around the age level of twelve or thirteen. An estimated eighty per cent of adult readers find it difficult to apprehend a dependent clause (a fact long familiar to the copy editors of advertisement agencies, magazines, trash fictions, and federal or state regulations). Because it is no longer a natural, immediate part of our schooling, reading in the full sense of referential recognition, of grammatical confidence, of focused attention will have to be taught as a particular art. Anyone who has tried to teach literature or history or philosophy to the average high school graduate will testify that this is what the job is all about. It can well be argued that reading in the full sense was always the prerogative of an élite, that our pictures of a lost literacy are idealized and never applied to more than an educated minority. But this does not infirm the case. That minority held the centers of power and of example; its criteria were those of the culture as a whole. This is no longer true. It is far more honest and far more productive to admit that the standards and ideals of a full literacy are not self-evident, that they are not applicable to the majority in a populist society, that they represent a special skill. We do not, after all, demand that all citizens be trapeze artists. What we must try to see to, is that those who *want* to learn to read fully can do so and that they be allowed the critical space and freedom from competing noise in which to practise their passion. In our fantastically noisy, distracted milieu this minimal room for private response is not easily come by.

These guesses and provisional suggestions may seem pessimistic. They are not meant to be. There is a strong element of health in our diminutions. Too much has been printed; too much made glossily available. Lincoln or Carlyle tramping miles to read and to excerpt a book provide an image to think about; as does Edwin Muir, new from the world of the crofters, chancing at an Edinburgh bookstall on the worn copy of *Zarathustra* which was to transform his inner and outer life. Because it has been made so easy, our sense of the act of reading has often grown facile. At the very outset of the centuries of high literacy, Erasmus tells of stooping in a muddy way to snatch up a torn piece of print, and of his cry of wonder and good fortune at the event. Tomorrow's bookmen may, perhaps, find themselves in a like condition. This would not be, altogether, a bad thing. . . .

Chapter 14

is print dying?

Ben Bagdikian

It is possible to imagine the reaction of the scholar of 200 B.C., used to scrolls of papyrus with a maximum extended length of twenty feet, to the suggestion that a modern large library would be practical. When he wanted to refer to a written work, the ancient scholar had to locate the scrolls and then unroll each one and read from the top to find the desired information. If he had been told that he would have to find a particular piece of information in a twentieth-century library consisting of 100 billion words on 300 million pages, in a million-volume library, it would stagger him. To find the desired information could take 690 years of continuous reading. But using the library's card catalogue to locate the one desired book among the million and then using the book's index to find the one desired page might take from a few minutes to an hour. As libraries become larger and men busier, even that is a tedious process, but it effectively overcomes much of the disparity between the masses of available printed information and the ability of the human eye and brain to locate a single item within the mass.

A man can deal with a computer in analogous ways to eliminate what he does not want. The human brain is far richer in its associations and syntheses than any conceivable electronic model of a brain. But a computer does some things better: it can repeat itself exactly when asked to; it will permit itself to be studied meticulously and at length to test its logic, knowledge, and truthfulness; it will do what-

"Is Print Dying?" from Ben Bagdikian, *The Information Machines* (New York: Harper & Row, Publishers, Inc., 1971), pp. 197–205. Copyright © 1971 by The Rand Corporation. Reprinted by permission of Harper & Row, Publishers, Inc.

ever it is instructed to do; and, if its instructor knows what he is doing, it will do it reliably under almost any circumstances.

When a computer places a message onto a TV-like screen, the viewer, if he has a keyboard or other device for querying the computer, can stop it and ask what it means or what basic data support a statement, or ask it to stop for a moment and pursue in depth one point the text made in passing. Or he can tell it to skip this subject and go on to another. Thus, though the eye can process only twenty characters per second of the text the computer presents, the viewer can use the computer's million-characters-per-second speed to search out and present only those characters the eye wishes to behold.

And the computer can do all of this without the use of paper, except for the portions of the total information the viewer wishes recorded and preserved in a document. Instead of multiplying shelves of books or the rising stacks of magazines, or the accumulated sheaves of newspaper, a simple switch dissolves the words on the electronic screen. The information in the computer remains intact, recallable at will, without an inexorable proliferation of paper.

The physical space being occupied by published documents is being reduced by another technique, microfilm, preserving the printed word in miniature on film.

At present microfilms are used in a number of variations. Microfilm is available in most libraries, usually in 35-mm. or 70-mm., often for past files of newspapers and magazines, their reels stored the way books are, read by threading them through a projection machine.

Later contemporary forms are microfiche, a sheet of film, usually four inches by six with sixty images on each sheet; and the aperture card, a computer data card with its rectangular holes bearing frames of microfilm. Recent developments in ultramicroform permit reductions of pages of two hundred to one, permitting thirty-two hundred pages on a four-by-six-inch transparency. If ultramicroform is used, a million-volume library will occupy the space of a small closet. A library of a million printed and bound books would cost about $30 million; the same library in ultramicroform would, if adopted for a large number of locations, cost less than $200,000, including the cost of machines for projecting the miniaturized texts.

Microforms of one kind or another are already in large-scale use, sometimes for business records and sometimes as a substitute for books and periodicals. It is estimated that in 1970 the production and operation of microforms was a $500 million industry. Already one of every five "documents" distributed by the federal government is a microform instead of a printed piece of paper. About 70 percent of all documents published by the Atomic Energy Commission in 1967 were available only in microfiche. The largest user of microfilm in the world is the Social Security system, which puts 30 million documents on film each year and destroys the originals, and handles a total of 168 million accounts through microfilm and magnetic tape. The Internal Revenue Service microfilms revisions of 90 million tax returns and distributes them to regional offices in that form.

The miniaturized text can be produced on film remotely by a cathode ray tube, a highly refined television tube, whose images are produced by a computer. One firm produces such microform at the rate of two thousand frames an hour, each frame indexed so that the computer can, if necessary, revise the information it originally implanted, and can also call it up for rapid display.

In 1969 the National Cash Register Company, which once made machines that did simple addition of dollars and cents, announced that it would begin selling books in ultramicrofiche.

Conceivably books, periodicals, and newspapers could be flashed on demand onto home or neighborhood screens, where a microfilm would be made in a small index-card-sized transparency capable of carrying texts and pictures equivalent to four hundred newspaper pages. High costs and the absence of mass systems make home use of this technique impossible in the near future, but it is a technique that works and could result in future alterations in the ratio between documentary and nondocumentary information in the home.

The commercial use of computers to select and print information at the demand of individual consumers is already at hand. The Encyclopaedia Britannica has stored the entire text of its twenty-volume *Annals of America* series in computer form; articles and data can be revised and brought up to date electronically without the typing-and-printing-and-page-proof routines that now are time-consuming and expensive. The Britannica computer has twenty-two hundred articles stored in it. It will offer school districts abstracts of each article, from which each school will order its desired full articles for its own custom-compiled textbook.

So the accumulation of information in print may very well change radically, including the display of news. There is already a massive intake of daily news through radio and television that uses no document and leaves no permanent record, and this has already conditioned the nature of what is printed in newspapers. There will be growing shifts in what is best displayed momentarily on a screen or some other ephemeral medium and what the consumer wishes to have in a document. But it will not be a simple substitution. If present patterns continue, the wider choice of electronically displayed news will whet the appetite for printed information, and in some cases will intensify the desire for related information reproduced in permanent form. Interest in printed stock-market returns in newspapers seems not to have diminished in those cities where instantaneous stock-market quotations are available on television channels. Before President Kennedy instituted live television press conferences a maximum of three newspapers in the United States printed substantial excerpts of the transcript. One year after the televised conferences had been established, forty-six papers were regularly printing substantial excerpts of the verbatim conference.

Thus, the rise of new electronic media will undoubtedly reduce the ratio of printed to nonprinted information, presenting more images without documents. But the assertion that "the tyranny of print" is ended and that sentences and paragraphs will be displaced almost entirely by nonverbal forms has no basis in present trends or in appreciation of how men think and learn. A permanent record will always be wanted, to permit comparisons with past and present, and to let different individuals interpret for themselves society-wide laws, warnings, instructions, accounting, and speedy comparisons of a wide variety of data. Record keeping, diaries, bookkeeping, mathematics, chronologies, and histories may be adaptable in part to nonverbal images, but for most of them words are quicker and more efficient.

Modern civilization depends on standardized words. It is no accident that the adoption of the Semitic alphabet, reducing all spoken sounds to about twenty-two basic letters, accompanied the rise of Greek logic and philosophy. Using more individualistic symbols makes universal communication almost unmanageable. The oral tradition depends on tone of voice, facial expression, posture of body, personality of the speaker, and attitude of the listener. It is a rich and necessary tradition, but it is ephemeral. Development of the Semitic alphabet was one of the most stunning inventions of man, learnable in a relatively short time and applicable universally without the alterations that come from random personality. The written word gave men a medium that permitted them to express those things that are precise and long-lasting, and that stand apart from unique emotion. It led directly to the growth of logic. If the symbols for an idea or for a body of information remain the same regardless of who prints them or reads them, and if these constant symbols continue to have meaning for a wide variety of people over a period of time, men can judge the universal significance of these abstractions. Without them, history is impossible, because there is no continuous expression that is not substantially altered by the most recent narrator and listener. Nor is there logic, since there is no way to repeat uniformly the steps by

which some individual came to a conclusion, and to do this consist-
ently among different persons in widely separated places.

There are, of course, ways of presenting ideas and human situations in graphic form—plays, movies, art—that are transportable and
repeatable. Their human meaning is profound. It is inevitable and
good that through history sensory and emotional activities should
challenge abstractions and universal assumptions. The abstractions do,
in fact, have an inherent danger of inhibiting individualism and sup-
pressing that part of the human personality that is not and should
not be entirely intellectual. But the fact that electronics has strengthened the power of the nonverbal and that some of this is beneficial
has led to a naïve dogma of the manifest destiny of multisensory
media. Some of it is not beneficial, since sounds, forms, and other
nonverbal sensory reproductions can be used for manipulative evil
purposes and can lead to suppression of individuality and personal
sensitivity just as print can. And the existence of richer and beneficial
sensory activities does not cancel the need for print as a medium
peculiarly adept at transmitting precise, rational, and consistent information.

The cult of the nonverbal is not only romantic in its dismissal of
words as a basic human communication and in its exaggeration of
print's artificial nature. But it also ignores a similar arbitrary restriction in nonprinted expression. The oral tradition has its own severe
limitations. The human being can make uncounted thousands of
different sounds through the manipulation of his breath drawn in and
exhaled, altered by the chest, throat organs, tongue, mouth shape,
and lips, plus mechanical sounds in these organs and tongue-and-teeth,
plus simultaneous movement of head and body. But nearly all language—including the oral tradition—has reduced these to about forty
sounds. The Semitic alphabet created twenty-two symbols (plus or
minus a few for variants like English) whose combinations roughly
approximate the forty sounds. The oral tradition, like the written,
would quickly break down if the several thousand sounds were not
standardized down to forty forms in order to let individuals and communities communicate with each other. "The tyranny of print" that
turned human expression into visual symbols, has its counterpart in
the "tyranny of syllables" by which primitive man became the speaking human being.

Furthermore, facial expressions and bodily gestures are not universal, but vary from culture to culture. These eventually will become
standardized as men have widening contact with each other. "Natural" gestures, for example, have different meaning for different cul-

tures. In the United States, pushing the hand, palm outward, forward and down, means "get away from here," while in some European countries and Latin America the same gesture means "come here." As Americans and Europeans increase communications with each other, in person and through electronic media, inevitably there will be standardization of "natural" communications.

Print, while never forgetting, has taught the mind to ignore it when it wants to. In a newspaper-reading test in Des Moines, two facing pages were printed, one having material almost exclusively of interest to women, the other for men. It was impossible to look at one page without being exposed to the other. About 90 percent of the women afterward reported opening the women's page and about 90 percent of the men their page. But 40 percent of the men said they never opened the women's page, though they had to in order to see the men's page. So, though print is cumulative and long-lasting, the human brain has defenses against unwanted print.

Reading continues to be the most intensive method of absorbing formal information.

In the late 1950s, after television had become a nearly universal phenomenon in the United States, Richard L. Meier calculated how much time urbanized Americans spent in various information-absorbing activities. Television clearly occupied more time than any other single method. In millions of person-hours a year he showed this time spent:

Television	6000
Lecture and discussion	4000
Reading	4000
Observation of environment	3000
Radio	1500
Films	160
Miscellaneous	5000

But, if the various methods are calculated not on simple time spent but on the amount of formal information received per minute, the order changes. Meier calculated the number of bits—the smallest unit of meaningful information—received by a single human being. In conventional information theory a bit is counted as one regardless of how many people absorb it, but Meier abandons this in calculating impact, so that each bit is multiplied by the number of individuals who absorb it. His estimated receiving rate of bits per minute received by an urban person for the various media are:

Reading	1500
Films	800
Television	400
Radio	300
Lecture and discussion	200
Observation of environment	100
Miscellaneous	100

Thus, for every minute spent at information activities, reading is almost double the "efficiency" of the nearest competitor, films, and $3\frac{1}{2}$ times more efficient than its most famous competitor, television.

This calculation is solely of formal information, without taking into account the quality or impact of any particular bit. The differing quality of each bit is plainly important in human affairs. Reading is fifteen times more efficient than "observation of the environment" in transmitting specific information, but perceptive observation of humman beings can obviously be more informative and more deeply moving than reading a psychology text. The point is not to suggest that information received by reading is always "better" or more significant. Sometimes it is and sometimes it isn't. But it is clear that the printed document is too efficient for some categories of information to be replaced by any medium yet in view. Among these categories of information in which print is superior is systematic, sequential information containing enough detail to make it beneficial for the reader to absorb it at his own speed and make selective visual comparisons between different statements within the adjacent documents. This covers a wide range of contemporary print, including detailed and analytical news stories, as well as more concentrated technical and scholarly work.

New methods of communication usually create new cultures, disrupting old assumptions and causing revolutions. This fact has led many to the conclusion that the electronically transmitted moving picture is peculiar not only in its graphic power but also in its ability to upset traditional ways, as demonstrated in the civil-rights and student rebellions in the United States in the 1960s.

"A great many individuals found . . . so many inconsistencies in the beliefs and categories of understanding handed down to them," we read in one commentary, "that they were impelled to much more conscious, comparative and critical attitudes to the accepted word picture, and notably to the notions of God, the universe, and the past."

This fits the assertion of believers in the uniqueness of the impact of television and other multimedia techniques to produce race riots, student rebellions, and the "generation gap." But the quoted passage is not about television. It describes the introduction of formal written words by abstract alphabets twenty-five hundred years ago, with new ideas and insights overturning the ancient values that had previously been preserved by a strictly oral tradition.

Print is neither dead nor dying. It is being forced to make a place in the family of human communication for a new way of transferring information and emotion, the electronic reproduction of scenes and sensations. The new medium is disrupting and even revolutionary, but it leaves the alphabet and document still indispensable to the efficient use of eye and brain and to the demands of human rationality.

Chapter 15

not since Babel

Edmund Carpenter

We know almost nothing about the origin of language. Anthropologists don't always admit this to undergraduates, but among themselves (when they're not trying to impress anyone) they acknowledge that we don't know whether language dates from a million years ago, or half a million, or fifty thousand. There are lots of theories, but few facts—and the facts fit lots of theories.

It was once rather loosely believed that man was an alienated ape who, after becoming erect, commenced talking. This early walkie-talkie roamed several continents, producing pebble tools that remained nearly changeless for hundreds of thousands of years. Then, less than fifty thousand years ago, man burst forth with a plurality of tools and art that presupposed, it was assumed, the existence of fully-developed language.

Today it all seems more complicated, largely as a result of new fossil discoveries, as well as the findings of ethology and somatology. It has recently been suggested, for example, that language emerged from a wordless but not soundless ritual, like Eliot's, "The word within a word, unable to speak a word/Swaddled in darkness." Alan Lomax, from the study of ethnic music, concluded that song is "danced speech." Bess Hawes found that the underlying principle in the songs of the Sea Islander is the unheard beat—like an orchestra in which nobody plays the tune because everybody hears it. The underlying beat is a motor beat. The music is a dance executed while standing still.

From Edmund Carpenter, "Not Since Babel," *ETC*. XXVII, No. 1 (March 1970), 67–74. Reprinted by permission of the International Society for General Semantics.

Some of the undergraduates I teach in California—especially the more intelligent ones—remind me, in their incapacity for formal speech, of Lancelot Andrewes' "The Word, and not to be able to speak a word." Either they stand mute, with all the dumb pathos of inarticulate farm animals, or they stammer, their faces twisting, like aphasia victims. What's called illiteracy is not ignorance of meaning, but non-sensitivity to word arrangements.

This retreat from language is surely one of the more interesting phenomena of our time. As George Steiner points out in *Language and Silence,* the syntheses of understanding which made common speech possible no longer work today. Large areas of meaning are ruled by non-verbal languages such as mathematics or symbolic language. Little or nothing is "verbal" in modern music or art. Both are languages, yet nothing can be said of either that is pertinent to the traditional habits of linguistic sense. When we ask the contemporary artist to explain himself, he refers us back to his work. He is reluctant to translate his efforts into words—that is, into a wholly different medium. Contemporary music also flies from exterior meanings. Language today deals only with surfaces of experience. "The rest," says Steiner, "and it is presumably the much larger part, is silence. The space-time continuum of relativity, the atom structure of all matter, the wave-particle state of energy are no longer accessible through the word. Reality now begins outside verbal language."

Not since Babel have words and thoughts clashed in such protesting combination.

The current situation is complicated even more by the rebirth of ritual which, though its origins are seemingly more ancient than language itself, lay dormant for 2500 years under literacy.

Both preliterate and postliterate ritual are highly involving, and what involves, surrounds. Thus it's not enough to say of x-ray art that it shows both inside and outside of a figure simultaneously. The question is, what does it mean to go right *inside* a form—to be "in the belly of the beast"? I suspect it's something like Alice going through the looking glass, or a Zuni patient stepping into a sand painting, rolling in it, as it were. One enters, becomes one with, what is portrayed. One goes right inside and takes over temporarily. One comes to know a thing by being inside it. You get an inside view. You step into the skin of the beast, and that, of course, is precisely what the masked and costumed dancer does. He puts on the beast.

Much the same may be said of the electronic environment where we are constantly bombarded by light images emanating from the cathode tube—Joyce's "Charge of the Light Brigade"—playing on us, going inside us, making us all the "Lord of the Flies," engulfed by flickering images.

"People don't actually read newspapers," says McLuhan, "they get into them every morning like a hot bath." The breakfast-reader, like the subway-reader, uses his newspaper as a wrap-around environment: he steps into the news.

Such art is "put on" art. It's the experience of entering a Bridget Riley walk-in, or a Light Happening ("Step right in," begins Allan Kaprow), or a tribal ritual where everyone participates *in* art. "When I am *in* my painting . . . ," said Jackson Pollock.

At most, words play only an integral part of ritual; at times they get in the way. Certainly ritual is not ordered and ruled by words or the grammars of either speech or print.

Artists, poets, children, tribesmen, film-makers find it much easier to accept the term "wordless thinking," when applied to ritual, than do scholars who will admit to two languages only: verbal and mathematical. For them, the analytical mode of thought alone is synonymous with intelligence. They are reluctant, for example, to grant dancers membership in a college faculty. But the knower as observer and the knower as actor behold different worlds and shape them to different ends, and it's senseless to condemn one for failing to meet the standards of the other.

Speech, emerging from ritual, retained much of ritual's multisensory character. In the tribal world, where the eye listens, the ear sees, and all the senses assist each other in concert, speech is a kind of web, a many-layered symphony of the senses, a cinematic flow which includes all of our "five and country senses." Eliot reminds us of this when he says a word can be a poem.

"Writing," says McLuhan, "meant a translation of this many-layered concert into the sense of sight alone. Reading and writing in this respect represent an intense degree of specialization of experience. Writing meant that the acoustic world, with its magic power over the being of things, was arrested and banished to a humble sphere. Writing meant the power of fixing the flux of words and thought. Writing permitted analysis of thought processes which gave rise to the division of knowledge. With writing came the power of visually enclosing not only acoustic space but architectural space. And before writing all of these divisions were merged into a single knowledge, a single rhythm in which there was no present but all was now."

Yet manuscript culture still retained some of the qualities of oral speech. Nothing was more alien to medievalism than silent reading. Reading was aloud, often as song, with gestures, usually performed while standing. Physicians sometimes prescribed reading as a form of exercise. Carrels were like telephone booths, designed to keep down noise.

Patients who have undergone throat surgery are forbidden to read, for there is a natural tendency for a reader to evoke absent sounds, and his throat muscles work silently as he scans the page.

A child learns to separate senses when he learns, in class, to read silently. His legs twist, he bites his tongue, but by an enormous *tour de force* he learns to fragment his senses, to turn on one at a time and keep the others in neutral. And so he is indoctrinated into that literate world where readers seek silent solitude, concert-goers close their eyes, and gallery guards warn, "Do no touch."

Print accelerated what writing began. The eye was no longer simply primary: with print it became dominant. This visual emphasis was two-fold: the nature of the eye is such that it fragments the field of observation; it favors one-thing-at-a-time; it isolates one element out of that total field and focuses on it, abstracts it out, forcing all else into the subliminal. It shatters the polysyllabic patterns of oral language into minimal, specialized units—into "words," which are essentially visual, spatial units.

There's a second factor: the eye emphasizes observable, measurable material things, and deals with their external surfaces, their outer appearances. The nonmaterial was translated linguistically into the material: such psychological states as tendency, intensity, duration were expressed as spatial metaphor: we said, "I can't *come* to *grips with* your argument, for its *level* is over *my head,* our *views* being so *far apart* my imagination *wanders,*" etc.; "thenafter" became "thereafter," etc.

Speech imitated print, and language retreated further from ritual. Step-by-step, language cast off its ritualistic features. It divested itself of all sensory connections, save sight, which it used in a highly specialized, restricted way: the eye of the marksman; the eye of the man holding a fixed position ("from where I stand"), having a "point of view," reviewing all experience, like Stalin reviewing troops or Milton reviewing life.

As late as the Renaissance, it was still possible to believe that language could enclose within its bounds the sum of human experience, at least human sensate experience. Mathematics was still anchored in material experiences which in turn, were ordered and ruled by language. But with the formulation of analytical geometry, the theory of algebraic functions, and the development of calculus, mathematics ceased to be a dependent notation, an instrument of the empirical, and became an autonomous language, totally untranslatable into speech.

Mathematics allowed man to escape from the spiral of language. "Language," says Steiner, "yields nothing except a further image of itself. It's an elaborate tautology. Unlike numbers, words do not contain within themselves functional operations. Added or divided, they give only other words or approximations of their meanings." Mathematics broke out of this circle.

Beginning about 1900, science shifted away from the empirical to the invisible. The concern, for example, was not with how calcite looked, smelled, or felt, but how it reacted to hydrochloric acid. Buckminster Fuller writes: "In World War I industry suddenly went from the visible to the invisible base, from the track to the trackless, from the wire to the wireless, from visible structuring to invisible structuring in alloys. The big thing about World War I is that man went off the sensorial spectrum forever as the prime criterion of accrediting innovations. . . . All major advances since World War I have been in the infra and the ultrasensorial frequencies of the electromagnetic spectrum. All the important technical affairs of men are invisible. . . ."

Even government has become invisible. We speak of the CIA as the "invisible government." What could be more natural in a society where truth is regarded as invisible, inner structure? In personal terms, the inner trip now supplants outer travel. It's the psychic leap man has been performing in this century. We no longer think of reality as something outside ourselves, something there, to be observed, measured. This concept came with Greeks, with literacy, and it goes with literacy, with the coming of the electronic media. Once more, after an interval of 2,500 years of literacy, reality is conceived as being within one, and the search for truth has once more become an inward trip.

Language plays little part in the inward trip. Words get in the way. Silence is regarded as a higher state, beyond the impurities and fragmentation of speech, free of the naive logic and linear conception of time implicit in print.

The application of mathematics in science, coupled with a concern with inner structure, led scientists away from the empirical and hence away from language. Today, chemistry is largely mathematical; genetics, almost wholly so. Increasing areas of biology are being taken over by mathematics. *The Origin of Species* is now regarded as essentially literary. Darwin and his contemporaries were concerned with outer appearances: how turtles *looked*. No wonder it took 35 years for them to understand the significance of Mendel's discovery.

Numbers are used in still another way: as neutral alphabet. Let me give a simple illustration; the first English census was called the Doomsday Book, not because it was used for taxation, but because its entries were visual, not verbal. "John Smith," written, lost many levels of meaning which "John Smith," spoken, retained; and this threatened the sense of identity of many people. When telephone companies dropped the prefix, as in GRanite 71111, and substituted 4771111, many people were resentful, for they found numbers, which didn't evoke an auditory image, more difficult to remember. People often feel a loss of identity when they are designated by number rather than by name; they say, "My name is 'John Smith,' not '47862.'" In this context, numbers aren't used as numbers but as neutral alphabet, totally devoid of all sensory associations.

Art and music, of course, cannot escape the sensate world; both are permanently tied to the senses. But neither is permanently tied to language. We could say of Rembrandt's work: this is a portrait of a man with a golden helmet. "But," says Steiner, "absolutely nothing that can be *said* about a Franz Kline painting will be pertinent to the habits of linguistic sense. A De Kooning canvas has no subject of which one can render a verbal account. It bypasses language and seems to play directly on our nerve ends." Art has ceased to be *re*-presentational; it no longer strives to create an illusion of being more than itself. It's a *thing*, to be responded to directly.

The same can be said of contemporary music, especially electronic music. Contemporary music isn't background music; it's foreground music: it engages our senses directly and requires our participation.

As we become increasingly tribalized in art and outlook, and draw closer to the Eskimo and Trobriander, anthropologists lose their best tool—the comparative method: its built-in shock, its challenge. My notion is that for the truly alien we must now turn to literature: Tolstoy, Hawthorne, Melville; we must say to students, "This is strange but it's human and it's worth knowing."

History is full of delightful reversals, where the opposite of what one predicts comes true. Where does the Word, where does literacy, survive in this vastly confusing Tower of Babel? My guess is that it may survive among drop-outs. In California, bookstores are feared as subversive centers; the underground press is written by and for drop-outs; the Word, not film, has become the medium of dissent. The hippies have discovered print, something totally new to them, and they are obviously thrilled by it. They discovered it outside their homes and outside their schools. They may not be able to express themselves very clearly as yet, but they have turned to literature—to classics, in fact—and it's possible the whole thing may turn out to be more than a put-on. Certainly print has proven an effective weapon in the hippies' search for identity through protest. Literature may survive as a result of their growing involvement in it. In contrast, the classroom presupposes an audience totally ignorant of all literary traditions: I recently saw a memo from a college textbook editor explaining that Joyce and Pound would have to be identified. We live in a scene where a large percentage of college presidents come from physical education, but drop-outs read Elizabethan verse and Greek drama.

When Constantinople fell, its scholars fled West, carrying their manuscripts with them. To read them, Western scholars had to learn Greek and thus they encountered not only Plato and Aristotle (hitherto known to them only through imperfect Latin translations), but a whole library totally new to them. This library, perhaps more than anything else, helped harness Renaissance technology to creative human ends.

Today's hippies are much like those fleeing scholars. They've taken the classics and fled from campuses which have fallen to weapon development, the CIA, and schools of social work. The notion that anything might come from this must appear, to school authorities, as wildly preposterous as the notion, to the conquering Muslims, that ragged monks with battered manuscripts were escaping with Constantinople's real treasures.

bibliography

Most of the following works contain extensive bibliographies that deal directly or indirectly with the impact of literacy, literacy and language, and literacy and other media.

PART ONE: the impact of literacy

Anand, Mulk Raj. "By Book or by Mouth," *Times Literary Supplement* (London), May 12, 1972.

Carey, J.W., and Quirk, James. "The Mythos of the Electronic Revolution," *The American Scholar* (Spring 1970).

Carothers, J. C. "Culture, Psychiatry, and the Written Word," *Psychiatry*, 22 (1959): 307–320.

Carpenter, Edmund, and McLuhan, Marshall. *Explorations in Communications*. Boston: Beacon Press, 1960.

Chappell, Warren. *A Short History of the Printed Word*. (A *New York Times* Book.) New York: Alfred A. Knopf, Inc., 1970.

Cipolla, Carlo. *Literacy and Development in the West*. Baltimore: Penguin Books, Inc., 1969.

Escarpit, Robert. *The Book Revolution*. New York: UNESCO Publications Center, 1966.

Finkelstein, Sidney. *Sense and Nonsense of McLuhan*. New York: International Publishers, 1968.

Goody, Jack, *Literacy in Traditional Societies*. Cambridge, Eng.: Cambridge University Press, 1968.

Havelock, Eric. *Preface to Plato*. Cambridge, Mass.: Harvard University Press, 1963.

Hoggart, Richard. *On Culture and Communication*. New York: Oxford University Press, 1972.

———. *The Uses of Literacy*. London: Chatto & Windus, Ltd., New York: 1957.

Innis, Harold Adams. *Empire and Communications.* New York: Oxford University Press, 1950.

———. *Minerva's Owl: The Bias of Communication.* Toronto: University of Toronto Press, 1951.

Kuhns, William. *The Post Industrial Prophets: Interpretations of Technology.* New York: Weybright and Talley, Publishers, 1971.

Lerner, D., and Schramm, W. *Communication and Change in Developing Countries.* Honolulu: East-West Center Press, 1967.

McLuhan, Marshall. *From Cliche to Archetype.* New York: The Viking Press, 1970.

———. *The Gutenberg Galaxy.* Toronto: University of Toronto Press, 1962.

———. *The Mechanical Bride: Folklore of Industrial Man.* New York: Vanguard Press, Inc., 1951.

———. *Understanding Media.* New York: McGraw-Hill Book Company, 1964.

Miller, Jonathan. *Marshall McLuhan.* New York: The Viking Press, 1971.

Ong, Walter J., S.J., *In the Human Grain.* New York: The Macmillan Company, 1967.

———. *The Presence of the Word.* New Haven: Yale University Press, 1967.

———. *Rhetoric, Romance, and Technology.* Ithaca: Cornell University Press, 1971.

Richetti, John. *Popular Fiction Before Richardson.* London: Oxford University Press, 1968.

Rosenthal, Raymond B. *McLuhan Pro and Con.* New York: Funk & Wagnalls Co., Inc., 1968.

Stearn, Gerald. *McLuhan Hot and Cool.* New York: The Dial Press, Inc., 1967.

UNESCO COURIER. January, 1972, July, 1972, and other issues.

Watt, Ian. *The Rise of the Novel.* Berkeley: University of California Press, 1957.

PART TWO: the crisis of literacy

Black, Max. *The Labyrinth of Language.* New York: Frederick A. Praeger, Inc., 1968.

Brockway, Thomas. *Language and Politics.* New York: D. C. Heath & Company, 1965.

Chomsky, Carol. *Acquisition of Syntax in Children from Five to Ten.* Research Monograph No. 57. Cambridge, Mass.: M.I.T. Press, 1969.

Chomsky, Noam. *Language and the Mind.* New York: Harcourt Brace Jovanovich, 1968.

Crews, Frederick. "Do Literary Studies Have an Ideology?" *PMLA,* 85 (1970): 423–28.

Dillard, J. L. *Black English.* New York: Random House, Inc., 1972.

Ehrmann, Jacques. "The Death of Literature," *New Literary History* (Autumn 1971), 31–47.

Gleeson, Patrick, and Wakefield, Nancy, eds. *Language and Culture: A Reader.* Columbus, Ohio: Charles E. Merrill Books, Inc., 1968.

Goodman, Paul. *Speaking and Language: Defense of Poetry.* New York: Random House, Inc., 1970.

Greenbaum, Leonard and Schmerl, Rudolf. *Course X: A Left Field Guide to Freshman English.* Philadelphia: J. B. Lippincott Co., 1970.

Grossman, Allen. "Teaching Literature in a Discredited Civilization," *Massachusetts Review* (Summer 1969) 419–32.

Hassan, Ihab, ed. *Liberations: New Essays on the Humanities in Revolution.* Middletown, Conn.: Wesleyan University Press, 1971.

Hymes, Dell. *Language in Culture and Society.* New York: Harper & Row, Publishers, 1964.

Kampf, Louis, and Lauter, Paul. *The Politics of Literature.* New York: Vintage Books, 1972.

Morse, Mitchell. *The Irrelevant English Teacher.* Philadelphia: Temple University Press, 1972.

Poirier, Richard. *The Performing Self.* New York: Oxford University Press, 1971.

Sledd, James. "Doublespeak: Dialectology in the Service of Big Brother," *College English* (January 1972). Rebuttals appear in *College English* (January 1973).

Sontag, Susan. *Against Interpretation.* New York: Farrar, Strauss & Giroux, Inc., 1964.

Steiner, George. *Extraterritorial: Papers on Literature and the Language Revolution.* New York: Atheneum Publishers, 1971.

——. *In Bluebeard's Castle: Some Notes Toward the Redefinition of Culture.* New Haven: Yale University Press, 1971.

——. *Language and Silence.* New York: Atheneum Publishers, 1967.

White, George, ed. "Literature in Revolution," *Tri-Quarterly* (Winter–Spring 1972).

PART THREE: the future: literacy and other media

Cheers, Colin. *On Human Communication.* Cambridge, Mass.: M.I.T. Press, 1966.

Disch, Robert. "Beyond Literacy." In *Affirmative Education.* Edited by Barry N. Schwartz. Englewood Cliffs, N.J.: Prentice-Hall, Inc., 1973.

Jennison, Peter S., and Sheridan, Robert M. *The Future of General Adult Books and Reading in America.* Chicago: American Library Association, 1970.

Licklider, J. C. R. *Libraries of the Future.* Cambridge, Mass.: M.I.T. Press, 1965.

Schwartz, Barry, ed. *Human Connection and the New Media.* Englewood Cliffs, N.J.: Prentice-Hall, Inc., 1973.